M000034633

Praise for *Collecting Courage*

"*Collecting Courage* is the first and only book that is brave enough to expose the poison that pervades our institutions, corrupts the corridors of power, fuels hate amongst its people, and allows injustice to flourish. But that's not its endgame. Each writer, by laying bare their pain, also expresses a special resilience through which they find love for oneself and community, create a space for healing, and invite everyone to rebuild a sector that sees its own truth and potential....**This book is a must-read** as you deepen your personal commitment to equity and social justice. It is a raw and honest chronicling of how racism, white supremacy and patriarchy permeate the world of charitable giving."

—**Dr. Krishan Mehta**, *The Charity Report*

"Each carefully woven piece carries a segment of a soul, lifts up the brilliance of a brain and gifts to you—the fortunate reader—an unforgettable collection of courage. Collecting Courage satisfies intellectual curiosities while teaching you how to silence negativity and rise above overt obstruction. Each account unleashes familiar feelings through a progressively compassionate prism. This read serves up relevant teachable moments. You will gain tremendous insights on how to empathize, enrich and empower underrepresented identities. This book is a treasured collection."

—**Tycely Williams**, *Advancing Philanthropy*

"*Collecting Courage* feels like a healing circle that gives space for discussion with colleagues who bravely share their hurts, their celebrations, and their hopes. It also reads like sitting in a master class with some of the continent's most successful fundraisers."

—**Raine Liliefeld**, *The Philanthropist*

"Two themes emerge from **Collecting Courage**. Firstly, racism towards Black fundraisers is historic and continues to this day, penetrating, poisoning, and polluting the charitable sector. Secondly, that by sharing the narrative of fundraisers who are Black and have experienced that racism can come unity, joy, freedom and love."

—**Rubin Kataki,** *The Charity Report*

"This book tells the truth. These 14 fundraisers, workers and leaders endured self-denial, self-doubt and injustice while striving and eventually achieving in the nonprofit world—while Black...It reads like an exposé about the evil tactics of enemies – the managers, leaders and co-workers, many who were oblivious to their own privilege and a few who were deliberate and aware, and chose to purposely dull the shine of their Black colleagues, knowing that there would be no consequence. Despite the challenges chronicled in the pages of **Collecting Courage**, the authors are one triumphant success story after another. They share intimate details about their own struggles to become leaders in the sector—directors, professors, executive directors, CEOs, CFREs, PhDs, MBAs and fundraising executives who have raised millions of dollars for some of North America's most prestigious schools and charitable organizations."

—**Ginelle Skerritt**, *Charity Village*

"In the last 10 years of writing what has amounted to thousands of blog posts, Richard and I have never promoted or reviewed a book… until today. Being middle-aged, white men, it's easy to go through life not realizing the privilege we've had and not having to think about our whiteness. This book brought us to our knees. It opened our eyes and challenged us to really think about what we can do as white male allies to bring racial and gender equity to our industry."

—**Richard Perry & Jeff Schreifels**, *Veritus Group*

COLLECTING COURAGE

Joy, Pain, Freedom, Love

Anti-Black Racism in the Charitable Sector

COLLECTING COURAGE

Joy, Pain, Freedom, Love

Anti-Black Racism in the Charitable Sector

Edited by:

Nneka Allen | Camila Vital Nunes Pereira | Nicole Salmon

Rootstock Publishing

Montpelier, VT

US Edition First Printing: 2021

Collecting Courage: Joy, Pain, Freedom, Love; Anti-Black Racism in the Charitable Sector
Copyright © 2020 Nneka Allen, Camila Vital Nunes Pereira, Nicole Salmon

US Release Date: 9/7/2021

Hardcover ISBN: 978-1-57869-065-7
Softcover ISBN: 978-1-57869-064-0
eBook ISBN: 978-1-57869-066-4

LCCN: 2021938204

Published by Rootstock Publishing
an imprint of Multicultural Media, Inc.
27 Main Street, Suite 6
Montpelier, VT 05602 USA

www.rootstockpublishing.com

info@rootstockpublishing.com

The original edition was published in Canada for worldwide distribution by
Gail K. Picco | Civil Sector Press 2020
Rootstock Publishing has licensed the book for a US edition only.

Editor: Jim Hilborn
Book design and production: Cranberryink

Printed in the USA

To our Black community, in all its diversity,
our truth, our stories are ours to tell.
Our voices are power.
We summon you to testify,
to document and to share your life.

Contents

FREEDOM

LOVE

Acknowledgments

OUR JOURNEY GETTING HERE

As editors, the opportunity to elevate the voices of Black fundraisers and professionals who collectively have 250 years of working experience in the nonprofit sector is thrilling to us.

Collecting Courage: Joy, Pain, Freedom, Love is a perfect example of what happens when two parallel paths converge to create something special and of significance. On one pathway was an initiative called *Our Right to Heal*, a feature about the experiences of Black Canadian fundraisers on the subject of healing published by Association of Fundraising Professionals (Global). The project was finally released a few days before George Floyd was killed at the hands of the police on May 25th, triggering worldwide outrage about police brutality against Black people and igniting protests against anti-Black racism.

On a related and separate path, our group of Black Canadian fundraisers had selected *Cap in Hand: How Charities are Failing the People of Canada and the World* by Gail Picco as our book club selection for December 2019. When Gail joined us for the discussion, she shared the idea she had of a compilation of writings featuring the voices of Black fundraisers. Then in March 2020 Gail became the Editor-in-Chief of a new digital magazine,

The Charity Report, and launched her own publishing imprint under Civil Sector Press.

Our two convergent paths had intersected, creating a perfect storm. Conditions and timing were right to address historic exclusion and oppression in the charity sector. In June discussions got underway about putting together a book, and *Collecting Courage: Joy, Pain, Freedom, Love* was born.

Gail — it is through your courage that we give life to this work. Thank you for being brave and for your willingness to speak truth to power. We love your sass! We are proud to be selected to be a part of the unveiling of Gail K. Picco Books.

Thank you to Jim Hilborn and Civil Sector Press for giving us space for Black voices to emerge to take centre stage in the charitable sector. Buckle up for this revealing journey. Our authors have spoken, and they have opened up and made public the inequities in the sector. This is a good starting point.

Introduction

NNEKA ALLEN

This is a collection and a documenting.

In it are the life stories of Black people. Black professionals who've spent the vast majority of their lives inspiring investment in social justice and change in the nonprofit sector.

We are Black fundraisers. And the reality is we live and work in the white world of philanthropy and charity. In these spaces, we are often the "first," the "only" and the "other." This "othering" links our experiences. We are bound together by our painful experiences of exclusion, denial and torment of anti-Black racism in our workplaces. But that isn't all that binds us together.

These stories reveal, in living colour, the love we as Black people cultivate, and the joy that springs forth despite our pain. They illustrate the freedom we carve out for ourselves through courage and community. To understand our vivid narratives, the historical truths that undergird our current reality must be laid bare, and to decipher our voices, the culture from which they emerge must be acknowledged and understood. From context comes understanding.

Before Europeans arrived in the late 15th century, First

Peoples, the Indigenous people, called North America Turtle Island. Europeans set about taking a wrecking ball to all indigeneity, killing, pillaging and colonizing First Peoples, and pitting Indigenous people against each other, ignoring tribal cultures and decimating sacred spaces. Meanwhile, they were also forging their merciless plot to traffic Black bodies across the Atlantic Ocean. Those Black hostages and their children became human fuel for the economic engine of what is today Canada and the United States.

The invaders brought their Spanish, French and British cultures with them, and for centuries, "settled" in various areas of the Continent. The English and French dominated, proclaiming the superiority of their cultures over Black and Indigenous peoples, and the English became the governing colonial force on the Continent until ousted by America in 1783.

Not so, however, in Canada, where the English settlers in Canada held dear to British colonial rule. Nor in Quebec, where the predominantly Catholic Quebecois in large number contested Protestantism and English colonial culture. The shared and prevailing cultures in this land, nevertheless, had become both French and English.

During the fervour of the 18th century's *Age of Enlightenment*, pseudo-science breathed life into the idea of the racial and cultural superiority of Europeans. It wasn't until then, when the European powers began mixing science and empire, that the idea of the supremacy of light skin over dark was created.[1] That idea of essential superiority laid the foundation upon which the culture of all of North America was formed. In fact, Canada and the United States share the same history and culture, and their national stories are inextricably intertwined.

North America is the world's third-largest Continent, beginning at the Arctic Circle and extending south to the Caribbean. No oceans divide the landmass, and the largest regions are the United States and Canada. Only in the last 174 years have these countries been separated by the 49th parallel—an arbitrary line born of politics and economics and in 1846 legally drawn by the Treaty of Oregon.

When the Europeans arrived in North America, there was no border to consider. People of shared backgrounds moved freely back and forth between countries, and loosely-controlled border checkpoints were not established until 1914. Otherwise, the rest of the extensive border remained unguarded[2] until the tragic events of 9/11 fundamentally impacted that liberty of movement.

Today, the 49th parallel notionally serves to separate two national cultures perceived to be distinct. One culture thought to be brash, bold and historically oppressive. The other seen as "nice," peacemaking and welcoming to everyone. Closer inspection of the history of this Continent, however, shows that, in the most important ways, the differences are actually more fanciful than real. In fact, they share the same imported dominant cultures, one landmass, an arbitrary border and the development of a massive economic engine—slavery.

The proliferation of plantation slavery in the Southern United States was a function of economics, geography and environment. Cotton transformed the American economy. The rich and fertile land of the South was perfect for such crops as cotton, tobacco and sugar, which drove the demand for more slaves.

The factors fostering the intense use of slave labour in the South did not exist in either the American North or Canada. Slavery is not defined only by a plantation economy. Societies in both the Northern U.S.A. and Canada found many profitable places for unpaid slave labour in homes, service businesses, mines, construction, factories and railroads — essentially throughout the entire economy.[3] Both Canadians and Northern Americans grew wealthy from the slave trade and investments in Southern plantations; as in the American South, personal property in slaves — *unpaid* labour — was a source of great wealth and prosperity for all.[4]

Few Canadians know there were 200 years of slavery in Canada at the same time slavery was raging in the southern part of the Continent. In 1834, the *Slave Abolition Act* ended slavery in the British colonies, including Canada. Contextually then, the 49th parallel was established 12 years after the end of slavery in Canada and 19 years before the American Civil War ended slavery in America. Thus, during the heyday of slavery in North America, American and Canadian slave-holding families, French and English, moved freely back and forth across the Continent with slaves in tow, some compelled by military events and others by residential preference. Families maintained homes and family in both the United States and Canada, a hallmark of the history of many of Canada's "notable" and wealthy families, many of whom share surnames and family connections with American slaveholders.[5]

Both countries were founded by the same people sharing the same cultures. The question then is, why is it that the United States and Canada maintain very distinct reputations and images today? Canada's identity is bound up in an odd and continuous colonial connection to the British monarchy. It aligns itself with the Crown as a point of pride and, perhaps, a matter of reputational necessity. It's a way to strategically distinguish itself from the United States[6] and from a history better known for its massive blood-stained history of slavery. And all the while large swaths of the Canadian population, not the least of which is Quebec, have maintained no special fondness for the English monarchy.

In fact, Canada shares fewer defining elements with Britain than with America. Whether by design or otherwise, the homage to Britain serves to obscure Canada's greater commonality with the United States, past and present. Canada shares the same blood-stained history. The people of Canada share a culture more closely tied both historically and traditionally to the United States than to Britain.

Why is this important?

Because the myths around American and Canadian culture must be demystified as we prepare to examine, through the writings in this book, the experiences of Black professionals in the charitable sectors of both countries. This is significant because the national context in which Canadian and American fundraisers live and work are more similar than not. And to fully honour and digest the stories shared in this book, we must begin by examining the fiction in both national narratives, and specifically dispel the myths that Canada is historically and socially superior and that Black people are better off in Canada.

The charitable sector is a microcosm of the national culture. In June 2020, *The Charity Report* noted that, "Charity leadership is almost exclusively white."[7] In Canada, as well as in America, not only do few Black people gain access to leadership opportunities, but also that access is often short-lived due to the oppressive and abusive work culture.

Benevolence, far from fully earned, is conferred gratis on the charitable sector. Its goodness is considered inherent, its intentions and image beyond reproach. But as with the Canadian image, the real identity and behaviour of the charitable sector must be subjected to the light of the truth. As has been the case with Canadian history at large, those who perpetuate the white saviour saga of the charitable sector have routinely erased the voices of Black people. Without the story of Black fundraisers, the documented history of the philanthropic sector will remain barren, incomplete, and given the current thrust of social justice, irrelevant.

A knowledge of these North American realities is critical when engaging with the lived experiences of Black people. These stories are sacred history in the making. They are truth and light. And they serve to correct the current philanthropic record. This is a collection of voices that have been systemically ignored and erased in a sector meant to promote the love of people. These are testimonies of the lives of Black men and women. Their stories are data, the stuff of primary source history.[8]

Fourteen writers from the United States and Canada. We write from the legacy of the same colonialism. The collaboration of the writers serendipitously created an expression of common realities in the charitable sectors in our respective countries. You will be struck by the similarities of our experiences. Our stories should be trusted even as they paint a contrasting picture of the charitable sector. These are the true circumstances in which we write and share the love we find in ourselves and our lives, even in the face of historic and continuing oppression, humiliation and ultimate rejection.

The deep source of our joy is a commodity. It defies our circumstances and is a life-preserver in the deep waters of anti-Black racism. The ability to cultivate joy in the face of pain is a generational legacy passed down through our DNA. Our intimate relationship with pain for over 500 years in North America is unparalleled. For centuries Black people have transformed pain into lyrics, music, poetry, dance and visual art for all of society. Our creative expression validates and affirms. It empathizes with all who suffer.

And freedom. This book is freedom. In it we are speaking the truth about our lives, with a hope that the minds and hearts of others will be transformed. With your heart open, walk with us as we unveil the courage we have collected in our lives and our profession. Despite devastating pain, our joy is effervescent and our desire for freedom insatiable. Our love endures.

Fragments

NICOLE E. COZIER

I move through the world in fragments,
Tripping over parts of myself along the way.
As each fragment jockeys for recognition, validation, and
acceptance,
I learn to quiet their clamoring voices like a nervous
parent quiets an exuberant child calling too much
attention to itself.
I contort my pieces to fit into spaces that were clearly
not meant for me.
The discomfort means I cannot stay long.
At the end of the day, I do a roll call to ensure all my
fragments are accounted for and none have been left
behind.
A comrade asks: "Who would you be in a world without
oppression?"
I answer: Whole.

JOY

CHAPTER 1

I Choose Joy

MARVA WISDOM

This is a deeply personal journey about *Joy*. It highlights the intersection of my religious evangelical upbringing and my later awareness of what my ancestors endured: imbuing obedience to prolong the slave and master relationship. It unveils the religious indoctrination that gave me a semblance of comfort and hope and was neatly wrapped up in the reward of future joy.

∞∞∞

"Joy, joy, joy, great joy. Joy, joy down in my soul."

Kirk Franklin penned these lyrics to the song *Joy* in 1992 while conducting the Georgia Mass Choir in a powerful rendition of the song. It became a part of my morning devotion. As a young girl in Jamaica, and as a member of our Pentecostal church choir, countless revival meetings and Sunday school gatherings were, similarly, not complete without singing *I've Got the Joy, Joy, Joy, Joy, Down in My Heart*, written by George William Cooke in 1925[9]. These two songs, written sixty-seven years apart, conveyed joy as an emotion, deep down in one's soul, in one's heart, attributed to a fervent religious experience.

During my first two decades on this planet, this is what I understood joy to be; seemingly present but inaccessible because it was deep down — to be sung about, talked about and celebrated, but only truly experienced in the afterlife when the Lord bestows it as a reward for being a 'good and faithful servant'. Obedient.

But joyful experience is not relegated to religious indoctrination. One of the most talked-about books of the 20th century, selling over 8 million copies to date, *The Joy of Sex*[10], focused not on the religiosity of joy but eroticism and pleasure. In the evangelical movement, however, this path of joy, at least publicly, is a path for sinners or to be experienced only within the sanctity of marriage, and then for the purposes of procreation, 'as God intended'.

The indomitable Audre Lorde in *Sister Outsider: Essays and Speeches* writes, "That self-connection shared is a measure of joy which I know myself to be capable of feeling, a reminder of my capacity for feeling. And that deep irreplaceable knowledge of my capacity for joy comes to demand from all of my life that it be lived within the knowledge that such satisfaction is possible, and does not have to be called marriage, nor god, nor afterlife."

In the shadows of my awakening as an adult, growing

away from my evangelical upbringing, I am embracing and deepening my understanding of joy. How colonial institutions, underpinned by Christianity, have enslaved and denied equity of opportunity to primarily Black and Indigenous people — purveyors of promised joy. What is most infuriating today is to see this same evangelical movement becoming more ideologically entrenched, and wielding political and economic influence with throngs of fervent followers, as it abandons the raison d'être of most religions: love, kindness, empathy, justice, truth and the inherent value of all human beings, 'precious in his sight'. And yet, so many evangelical leaders amass great wealth, power and influence, finding what they would see as comfort and joy, their reward on earth for being 'good and faithful servants'. Not waiting for the Lord to bestow theirs in heaven.

Yet while a significant number of its leaders continue to pollute our political system, ensuring that systemic and structural inequities remain intact and equal opportunity elusive, we the people must respond. Our ancestors paved the way through their sacrifice, and we have unprecedented access to information and tools needed to dismantle a system based on the promises of future joy in another realm. And still there are many within the religious community, including some evangelicals, that do believe in the importance of being charitable through service, whether it is food, comfort, hope, shelter and yes even spreading joy. It is through tithing and other philanthropic endeavours they meet needs because they see this as a vital part of their reason to exist. Feed the hungry, shelter the homeless, cloth the poor. As a collective or as individual members they are in the fight for social justice — sometimes on the front lines.

Sadly, there are still too many who use much of their privileged position, supported by the giving of the faithful, to uphold systems and structures that are anything but just. And unfortunately, many of us continue to support this type of religious community and leadership that propagates injustice and preserves the oppressive system that brought us slavery, pain, heartache and cultural annihilation. Quoting my fellow Jamaican, the iconic Robert Nesta Marley, "emancipate yourself from mental slavery, none but ourselves can free our mind."

How can we be so blind to the parallel of yesterday and today? How can we not hold our religious leaders accountable for the malaise that has gripped our society when they, with captive audiences, at least weekly implicitly accept or actively support an oppressive system, promising patrons — joy? In fact, we have been complicit in deeming religious leadership off-limits for public and political accountability. We have shielded them behind the pulpit while they wreak havoc on our societies as God's proxy in the sale of future joy purchased with our humble acceptance of current inequity.

Those who led the slave trade fought against civil rights, wiped out Indigenous populations and attempted to cancel cultures. These same folks now stand as the purveyors of what is 'right', the centuries-old argument that our reward is in heaven. But I for one demand my joy now! I do not need a proxy to help me find it. It need not be 'deep in my soul' or 'down in my heart'. It is best at the surface — attainable, accessible and activated. And further, I must speak up and speak out about the comfort I found growing up in my religious cocoon and how it is not serving society as God intended.

How then, do I travel this life's journey and better understand this theme of joy that is so very elusive to so many? Is this a sequel or a prequel to healing? Life has taught me what joy is not—fleeting, momentary, transactional, temporary, externally driven, accessed in the beyond. Further, it is not the opposite of pain, suffering and sadness. Perhaps then, it is neither a sequel nor a prequel.

Our ancestors survived in part because they found comfort and hope in the promise of future joy. Joy for me, however, is a choice for today. It is a state of being from whence comes the act of doing. Who we are, the state of being we choose and the actions or activities that follow allow us to surface the joy that lives within all of us.

Now, claim your joy!

►●◄

Marva Wisdom is a leading voice in Canada on empowering social change and a Senior Fellow at the Munk School of Global Affairs and Public Policy (University of Toronto).

CHAPTER 2

Discovering Joy

SHERRIE JAMES

It's 5:30! It's 'mommy time'! It's workout time.

The *Afrobeats* blasts through my television, and I start dancing. The day fades away. I'm in my happy place. I am present and I'm loving every minute of it. Before I know it, I've completed a dance workout. I was exercising and I don't feel it. Instead, I feel ready for whatever is to come. I feel relaxed. I am calm. I am joyful.

Not too long ago, I found the idea of exercise exhausting. Who would want to punish themselves in this way, especially after a long and stressful day at work? Was I insane for wanting to work out? I was often feeling sick and drained and felt I needed to get in shape. So I committed. I knew I could carve out a 30-minute window with my family, so I took it. I tried different workouts and found that I gravitated to workouts that included dance. Then I discovered the *Afrobeats* workout.

I did not know at the time that this 30-minute

workout would be nourishment for my soul. I did not know that dance resonated with me because I needed to reconnect with my childhood. I did not know that *Afrobeats* resonated because I needed that connection to my roots, the part of me that I have never taken the time to know — my Blackness.

All this started around April 2020. We were home isolating, social distancing and dealing with the uncertainties that came with COVID-19. I ate to comfort myself as I sat glued in front of the TV, and that's why I assumed I was feeling off. I needed to exercise. This, of course, was a manifestation of the worry and concern, the fear I was carrying. Then George Floyd died and the world took notice. I didn't. It was yet another example of the extinguishment of the Black man. This was our normal. But this time I was forced to take notice, because the rest of the world took notice. To put it candidly, I was forced to notice because the white people around me were reacting. They were upset. They were feeling guilt. Suddenly, the me who was already off had to go into overdrive, into a space I had never really visited before. Yes, I've been angry about racism. I've been a victim of it. But I knew how to survive. Brush my shoulders off. Don't overthink things. Get off the ground. Keep moving because 'ah got shit to get done'. I have people depending on me. I do not have to acknowledge it.

I am a fundraiser! I've made this profession my life's work for the past 18 years. I am a fundraiser! It is a title that I owned proudly for most of those 18 years. I was generous in helping others. This was my calling. To sacrifice. To become a martyr for whatever cause or mission or organization. In retrospect, it was my ego. I had created a perfect house for our sector in my mind because we fundraisers are the "good ones." We sacrifice. I put myself on a pedestal and called myself super. But there is something about being above everything and everyone — the crash back down to reality can be devastating, heartbreaking, demoralizing.

This attitude about sacrificing blinded me to the fact that I had become a doormat, a shell of myself. In my very first job, I worked with some wise women, women who had *lived*. They found joy in their work. They were committed to the communities they served and to the donors who made the work possible. They exemplified what working in the sector could be and should be. They were my inspiration. They wanted me to blossom and encouraged me to seek other experiences. With love and respect we parted ways. Soon after came my first revelation, the first crack in the wall. I could not find a job.

There was no doubt I bombed some interviews, but I also know that I excelled at others. After one of those positive interviews, I was introduced to a mover and a shaker in the sector, a well-respected older white man. And he gave me the most impactful advice that I've carried with me since: *"This sector is one of the most racist. Do not be fooled by the label charitable."* He helped me see more clearly, and for that I'm grateful. What happened next, however, set me up for a devastating crash down to reality.

Knowing that my skin was now a factor in my workplace, I taught myself to 'play' dumb in moments when I was being mistreated. And then I taught myself to be numb in the moments when the realization, the hurt and the pain, sunk in.

I am a fundraiser who did not want to acknowledge that my Blackness shaped my experiences. I was excluded from meetings and did not get to meet certain donors, yet my job description or my title would suggest otherwise. I got used to being the only Black person in the room and convinced myself that I was lucky to be there, that I was fortunate and I should rise to the occasion. I smiled. I told myself, I'm here, this is an opportunity, this is a moment to take advantage. Taking advantage, however, meant denying myself. I became someone who could melt into the walls at any moment. Assimilation became one of my greatest strengths. I sat back, observed, and adjusted 'who' I brought to work to fit in with my boss, my coworkers, my donors. And so I spent most of my 18 years withering away while reminding myself to be grateful. I am an immigrant after all. This country does not have to treat me this well. I have a full-time job. I have benefits. Suck it up, I am strong.

See, for as long as I could remember I knew I had to be a strong woman. Not a strong Black woman, just a strong woman. I grew up in Grenada, a country where people of my skin colour are the majority. I did not have to figure out how to navigate white supremacy. I had the freedom to simply be a little girl. And growing into a strong woman was a given because every woman around me was strong.

I grew up learning from three generations of women. My grandmother and two of her sisters lived within arm's length of each other — at times too close for comfort. Their daughters lived with them, and the granddaughters (my generation) became my best friends, my sisters. I saw women who were mothers and fathers. They were the breadwinners, disciplinarians, teachers. I saw my grandmother, my aunties, my mother all work tirelessly to provide for their families. They were warriors—constantly ready for battle. They were tough. They showed no weakness.

I spent my youth having fun, playing with my cousins, loving music and dancing. I was happy. I never questioned why my mother did not socialize much. I never questioned why my grandmother and my aunties were constantly taking care of others. I did not notice my mother feeling sad. I did not notice that she didn't laugh much, that she didn't seem to have hobbies. I had no idea what she liked. She was constantly focused on caring for her children, seeing us through every possible obstacle.

Today I see my grandmother, my aunties, my mother in me. Their strength has soaked every fibre of my being. I see them show up in how I care for my kids; I am a strong woman after all. But they did not prepare me for facing my Blackness. I did not prepare. And when confronted with it with, nowhere to run, I found myself breaking. I could no longer just brush my shoulders off. I was feeling weak. I could not go into battle every day and come out victorious, ready to face another day. It was too much! So I shut down.

In May 2020, the impact of George Floyd's death rocked my world. The outcries from my Black brothers and sisters from Minneapolis to Toronto tore into my being. The protests and reactions from around the world made visceral for me that my world was not real. The fundraising illusion I had built, the pedestal I had placed myself, and the nonprofit sector, on — shattered. There had always been cracks in the wall, but I had become pretty good at patching things up. I employed dumb and numb when I needed, and other times I ignored the aggressions and focused on how I could improve. But this…this was different.

I became withdrawn. I would cry for no reason. I would start my workday reading yet another email about Black solidarity and I wanted to scream! What does it mean? What are you *really* going to do now? I was standing among the shards of glass that was my idea of this sector and I was afraid to hope. I was afraid to take a step in any direction because I felt like the centre of my very being was empty, a lie. There is no equity. I had to respond to George's death. I had to be supportive of Black people. This was the only option. And being in the charitable sector made my participation even more urgent. We were just hit by a tsunami or maybe it was the perfect storm, but only Black people were being destroyed. Why did it have to take a tsunami? And what will happen when the waves subside? I would end my days quite negatively with this mantra — *this is just a moment, and it too shall pass.*

It was heavy. It is a heavy load being Black in fundraising, but I continued with my workouts. The power of 30 minutes! Dance brought the joyful little girl alive and the beautiful beats of the African music I listened to taught me that being Black is so much more than what was happening around me. I gave up and gave in to the energy, the vibes that came with the aerobics. The

30 minutes turned into an hour. I eventually recognized what I was feeling. Joy! And I wanted more.

I started to carve out more time for myself. It was no longer about getting in shape physically but mentally and emotionally. I had to let go of my image of a strong woman and begin to reshape what that meant. I don't just want to be like my mother or my grandmother; I want to be more; circumstances *require* me to be more! To continue to show up and go into battle I needed to recharge, I needed rest, I needed to see more than a battlefield ahead of me. I started listening to podcasts, I reached out to someone I felt I could trust for help. I started to do more with my kids—simple things like going for more walks and seeing the world through their eyes. There is nothing like the innocence of children. It is the cure, the healing of the unseen wounds. Before I knew it, I was learning to be present. To find joy in the little things. With this awareness came gratitude. I have so much to be thankful for, so much to be happy about. I am healthy and my family remains healthy. A slow peace has started to descend on me, a gradual acceptance of everything I am—enough.

Once I got to this point, I started to recognize the moments the universe had curated just for me. I wasn't the only one at work who was struggling. Every person of colour now had to navigate this messy world in a way they hadn't before. We were coming to grips with the reality that some of our colleagues have been—and remain—blind to their supremacy. We are conducting our own inventory and looking at how we treat each other, how we conform to fit in, to be more 'white'. We are helping each other to see, to hear, to feel the words and intentions of our white colleagues and how their actions were often a contradiction.

I now have a support group at work — a space where I can expose myself, expose the hurt I endured for most of those 18 years. A space where I am learning and connecting with my Black and brown colleagues as never before. I discovered that our experiences in this sector were at times shocking, yet at the end of every meeting I walked away lighter. I was not alone. I had voice. I had agency. These connecting points brought me joy in moments of deep despair without me even realizing it.

The universe, God, did not stop there. I was being blessed with gentle reminders that I have always been loved, not the strong woman, not the Black woman, just me. I have always been loved! I began noticing the random song that would pop into my head to make me smile, the 'just because' hugs I would get from my kids, the stranger at the grocery store who is kind to me for no reason, the cutest dog, or how good I felt after a shower. The things that I would often take for granted now interrupt my battles, brighten my day, make me question whether I need to be a warrior right now.

Finding joy should be intentional. As we seek justice or wealth or strive towards a goal, we must try to have joyful moments along the way.

Joy lightens the load.

Joy reminds us to be present.

Joy coats us and arms us for the battles to come and it can be our shield when we are weary.

I'm still discovering how I can be a strong Black

woman, but now it's because I want to be. I am still a fundraiser learning how to be smart in the moment and to be authentic. I am shedding the expectations of others and letting my little girl dance. I'm using the strength of the amazing women who raised me to fuel this path I am on. I'm embracing vulnerability as new armour, a tool to become even stronger. I'm continuing to be grateful for my blessings. And I'm enjoying this journey knowing I welcome what's to come. I'm ready.

►●◄

Sherrie James is a fundraising executive with more than 18 years' proven success in development, marketing, project management and event management. She is the new Director of Philanthropy for Luminato Festival Toronto and mother of two.

CHAPTER 3

The Epiphany of a Joyful Fundraiser

CHRISTAL M. CHERRY

"Something is wrong. It's probably you."

A friend told me this by phone while I was in the car on my way home. I had just told her I had been let go as the Chief Development Officer. Again.

I was quiet.

"Are you there?" she asked.

"Yeah, I gotta go," I said. "Talk to you later,"

She meant well, but her words hurt.

I came home and went straight to the bathroom. I thought I would vomit, but instead, I looked in the mirror. I cannot believe this has happened again. It must be me. I am not fit for this work. My thoughts were racing.

What else can I do? Become a teacher? A counselor? A crossing guard?

I laughed.

Even still, you are trying to help people.

My mind began to replay some recent events at work. And then a barrage of questions filled my brain: Why would he omit me from meetings? Why would he not acknowledge me at a meeting at my church that I scheduled with my pastor, who had invited other pastors in our denomination to hear about our mission? Why would he cut me out of a discussion that involved a donor I had been cultivating for a gift for eight months? Even the donor was confused, and she later called to ask me what was going on.

What *was* going on? What kind of leader acts this way?

I googled the word *fear*. Then I googled the word *leadership*.

I learned the elements of fear-based leadership included:

Lack of a vision, or refusal to make the vision clear to the team

Lack of transparency and obfuscation

Talking *at* the team, not with them

Not setting out values or standards of behavior

Blaming failures or lack of progress on external forces

Offloads on the team and blaming them for blunders

This was it!

It was consistent with what I experienced and had been experiencing for years.

I ran to my *Points of Pride* box where I kept all my

awards. One for outstanding leadership from the United Negro College Fund; a Certificate of Appreciation from the American Society for Public Administrators; a Certificate of Completion from Atlanta's United Way V.I.P. program; and certificates in Nonprofit Leadership, Nonprofit Management, and Nonprofit Social Media.

I read multiple notes I had kept from donors, alumni, college presidents, and volunteers, thanking me for caring about their passions and interests. I looked at evaluations from courses I taught, reminding me that I had done well. The box was full of accolades. I needed those affirmations.

Mild relief wafted over me. I had made an impact. But what now? I could not think.

I prayed and fell asleep.

While straightening my office a few days later, I fell upon one of my favorite books, *A Spirituality of Fundraising* by Henri J. M. Nouwen. It is a small, thin book, so I sat down to read it again. I turned to the first chapter after the acknowledgements, and it read, "*Make love your aim.*"(1 Corinthians 14:1, NJB). My shoulders lowered and I delved into his words until I came to my favorite part in the chapter:

> "*When we seek to raise funds, we are declaring that we have a vision that is amazing and exciting. We are inviting donors to invest through the resources that God gave them—their energy, their prayers, their money—in this work to which God has called us.*"

I grabbed my highlighter and marked these words in yellow for emphasis.

I kept reading,

"Whether we are asking for money or giving money we are drawn together by God, who is about to do a new thing through our collaboration."

I wrote "Hallelujah" in the corner of the page.

"Fundraising as a ministry." I googled it.

To my surprise, many resources popped up in the feed: *Growing Givers' Hearts*, *The Giver and the Gift*, and *Ask Without Fear for Christian Ministry*. I read the descriptions feverishly; I was convinced that nonprofit work pleases God. I knew I could not leave this sector but did not want to return to being on the front lines of fundraising. Inevitably you are quick to be a casualty if the wrong leader is at the helm…again, thoughts about leadership.

I remembered the faces of those in my classes I taught about major gifts. All nodded in agreement when I stated it is the *leaders*—the VPs, the CEOs, and even the board members—who really need to take these classes to understand all the nuances and needs of a vibrant and robust fundraising operation.

A few days later, over coffee with a few respected fundraiser colleagues in a downtown Atlanta restaurant, there were lots of eyes rolling, heads bobbing, and words of agreement:

"Sylvia was laid off last week, and Julia just straight quit because of her CEO. I heard Kylie was written up because she didn't meet the goal even though she had no resources and a sorry board."

That meeting of African-American women fundraising

minds in Atlanta would later become a more formal network, a safe place for women to share and laugh and cry when the writing on the wall made it clear their turn was next. And to this day, the *Fabulous Female Fundraisers* meet for virtual hugs (due to COVID-19) and to affirm that we have each other's backs. After I left my organization, my friends threw a party for me. They came with wine and music and wings and love, and the sting of having been let go was not as painful.

A couple of months later, as we were heading home from my ten-year-old son's check-up, he proudly ran to the front passenger side of the car. The doctor had confirmed that he was now eighty-two pounds — big enough and heavy enough — to sit in the front seat. Smiling from ear to ear and looking out the window as though seeing things from the front seat would be different, he rolled down the window and gazed up at the sky: "Mom, moving from the back seat to the front is proof that I am growing up and ready for the next level," he said.

"The next level?"

"Yup, being in the front gives me courage. I am ready to drive."

I smiled. Those words stayed with me long after we got home. I was moved but didn't know why. At 4:00 a.m., my eyes popped open.

The epiphany came to me.

I was allowing the fear, of *now*, to block the courage for *next*. I was still in the back seat! I was allowing others to drive for me and stunt my growth towards my destiny.

Something was wrong and it *was* me!

Things would need to change. I knew I could not

continue. I could not return to the back seat. I knew how to drive. I needed to grab some courage and move to the next level. I decided to take a leap of faith and stepped into the driver's seat headed straight to the top — to boards of directors — when I opened my firm, I called it *The Board Pro*.

I knew from sitting in long board meetings that many boards are clueless and apathetic to what truly happens inside the organization. Often, no real accountability happens with the CEO. Rosy stories and mission moments tend to cloud judgement and diminish a willingness to speak up when there is a gaping hole in the floor. Instead, everyone tiptoes around it, pretending it is not there. Reports with failing budgets in red and executive staff resignations, layoffs, and terminations often go unquestioned because the CEO controls the message. The board smiles and nods about the report as if everything is dandy.

In many cases I have seen, the CEO abuse executive power to cover up wrongful acts of negligence and poor leadership. My colleagues have left organizations in tears and bewilderment, knowing no lifeline would be available for those who would come next. A few times, to deaf ears, I tried to warn board members of the challenges we faced on the inside. I sat in the back seat and waited for my turn.

Today, in my work as a consultant, people want to hear what I have to say. I train boards to perform assessments of their performance and that of their one employee, the CEO. I can openly tell them *there is a problem and it is probably you*. So often, a board chair or executive director will thank me in private for saying to their board what he or she could not.

Finally, I can make a difference in a way that can have impact and be helpful to others who are in roles I formerly held. With board training and development, I remind board members that, as good stewards of mission work, they have a responsibility to lean in and get a good glimpse of the organizational culture they represent on the board and inside the nonprofit.

It feels good to hear a board chair say I *"lit a dormant fire"* that helped them spring into action to make a change in policies or to begin raising funds, or to receive feedback that someone in one of my webinars "felt blessed" because of something I taught. I had sat in the back seat for so long, painfully trying and retrying to do good work that would be beneficial for someone else. Because of my Christian faith, I believe that my life has meaning and that I am alive not only for me but for others. My struggles, my pain, and now my discovery is my testimony.

I have something to offer. My experience, my skills, my talents are needed. My pain was not in vain. It led me to my purpose!

After twenty-two years in this nonprofit space, the light has come on. I find joy in this work. Something is very right, and for sure, it *is* me.

Christal M. Cherry is the CEO of The Board Pro and on faculty at CANDID where she teaches courses in fundraising and board development. She earned an MA in Counseling from Hampton University, a BA in Liberal Arts from Hofstra University, and multiple professional development certifications. She currently serves on the board of the Greater Atlanta chapter of the Association of Fundraising Professionals and the Villages of Carver YMCA.

PAIN

CHAPTER 4

Come, Take a Walk With Me

NICOLE SALMON

*I shall pass through
this world but once.
Any good therefore
that I can do or any
kindness that I can
show to any human being,
let me do it now.
Let me not defer or
neglect it for I shall
not pass this way again*

—*Stephen Grellet, 1773-1855*

Nestled between the pages of the book of Psalms
in my late Mom's 'The New Oxford Annotated Bible'
this verse is written on worn beige card stock
upon which is an image of an open gate,
these words neatly inset. How it came into her possession
is unknown, with utmost care held in plastic sleeve,
a precious message it held.

This verse speaks to me
As if tucked away in the abyss of me
As if sucked into every cell and fibre of me
These words captivate and speak to me
Cause it is who I am and aspire to be

'tis Pain & Hurt
See

Accused of being angry, aggressive and intimidating,
body language, glances and glares signal Blackness in need of checking.
Warned to tone it down, tame our hair, don't take credit, don't say much.
When it's time to be seen and counted
a parade on the diversity red carpet we are invited.
A pat on the back, smiles all around, check mark the box,
keeping up appearances, an inclusivity must.

This verse speaks to me
As if tucked away in the abyss of me
As if sucked into every cell and fibre of me
These words captivate and speak to me
Cause it is who I am and aspire to be

'tis Pain & Hurt
Hear

Floating in on a subtle melody, a faint voice whispering,
collective calling...enticing, encouraging, ensnaring
bewitched, bothered and bewildered, hunger and desire like no other,
you are made for this, this is who you are...don't resist.
At what point did doing good stop feeling good anymore?
With injustice storming, a pin drop can be heard in the vacuum of your silence.
A voice on loop keeps urging us, "hold on cause you really do matter."

This verse speaks to me
As if tucked away in the abyss of me
As if sucked into every cell and fibre of me
These words captivate and speak to me
Cause it is who I am and aspire to be

'tis Pain & Hurt
Breathe

Amoebic body, moving with sticky fluidity, imposter syndrome,
where fitting in becomes a singular obsession, assimilation is like religion.
We tell ourselves, "educate, be twice as good, work twice as hard"
for the ultimate reward...to be valued half of what whiteness dictates.
Dual personas, hide ourselves, dull our shine, check our britches
holding on to keep a recognizable piece, a reminder of who we are.
Sucking thin air...breathe...just breathe.

This verse speaks to me
As if tucked away in the abyss of me
As if sucked into every cell and fibre of me
These words captivate and speak to me
Cause it is who I am and aspire to be

'tis Pain & Hurt
Taste

Tasted your wrath and sting of your venom
like so many others, been sliced by your actions and fragile reactions.
Gnashing teeth threatening to consume every part of me
like a sponge, soaking, absorbing, holding in poison
never spilling, suck, suck, suck it up,
medicate don't regurgitate...side effect
self-harm in full effect, physical and mental distress.

This verse speaks to me
As if tucked away in the abyss of me
As if sucked into every cell and fibre of me
These words captivate and speak to me
Cause it is who I am and aspire to be

'tis Pain & Hurt
Feel

Puffed up with unearned generational power
throwing and landing micro- and macro-aggressions by the hour
Black and brown bodies sliced and diced, high pain threshold is the lie sold.
Tiny cuts, deep cuts, cumulative harm and on bended knees,
confidence nurtured and gathered, stripped and laying in tatters.
Taking aim, you deliver a final blow
"Sorry you don't fit in and you are being let go." Fired!

This verse speaks to me
As if tucked away in the abyss of me
As if sucked into every cell and fibre of me
These words captivate and speak to me
Cause it is who I am and aspire to be

'tis Pain & Hurt
Unveiled

A sector holding closely to its charitable roots,
doing good deeds and serving those in most need.
Outwardly facing, on surface appearing,
all compassion and caring, purity and goodness overflowing,
but alas, that veneer is peeling. The story that's been told is incomplete.
Curtain-call reveals, secrets concealed, underbelly of injustices
borne on branches, supremacy of whiteness has taken firm root...even here.

This verse speaks to me
As if tucked away in the abyss of me
As if sucked into every cell and fibre of me
These words captivate and speak to me
Cause it is who I am and aspire to be

'tis Pain & Hurt
Break

A reckoning well overdue...now's the time for heeding advice.
Truth be told, 'The System' impotent can do no harm or deliver blows
without its enablers, defenders and those in comfort of complacency's arms.
'Cause as surely as it hurts 'Others' it's bamboozled self-anointed 'Belongers'
planting seeds of hatred sprouting white superiority
instead of seeds of equity and our shared humanity. Oppression and
exploitation doesn't have to be our final destination.

This verse speaks to me
As if tucked away in the abyss of me
As if sucked into every cell and fibre of me
These words captivate and speak to me
Cause it is who I am and aspire to be

'tis the Beginning and the End

My Sisters and Brothers in the trenches, continuing the fight
for what's just right, I pledge my presence walking side by side.
I know you — I see, I hear, I smell, I taste, I feel you.
In the marrow of my Blackness I am you.
The road we all travel is not solitary,
different pathways converge
into a linked, shared and the oneness of humanity.

This verse speaks to me
As if tucked away in the abyss of me
As if sucked into every cell and fibre of me
These words captivate and speak to me
Cause it is who I am and aspire to be

'tis Our Walk

Come, take a walk with me.
We need Courage to Walk Good in this life.

I shall pass through
this world but once.
Any good therefore
that I can do or any
kindness that I can
show to any human
being, let me do it now.
Let me not defer or
neglect it for I shall
not pass this way again

—Stephen Grellet

This verse speaks to me
As if tucked away in the abyss of me
As if sucked into every cell and fibre of me
These words captivate and speak to me
Cause it is who I am and aspire to be

►●◄

Nicole Salmon has over 25 years of fundraising and senior leadership experience. In 2014 Nicole founded Boundless Philanthropy. She currently serves on the board of two nonprofit organizations and is a member of the Canadian Black Fundraisers Collective.

CHAPTER 5

The Pain of Assimilation

MUTHONI KARIUKI

My career in the charitable sector began over ten years ago when I realized that I could make a difference through the power of philanthropy for causes and communities I am passionate about.

Fundraising has always been part of my life. I grew up watching my parents, who are fundraisers and philanthropists, helping people in our community. Our home was often the physical location for fundraising activities and events, where people would come together to contribute and raise money for everyday financial needs that existed within the community.

I learned early in my childhood that my African cultural identity was important to my parents. They wanted to ensure that I grew up understanding who I am as a Black woman in the context of my Kenyan culture. As I grew into adulthood, I never conceived of a scenario where my identity as a Black African woman would be threatened, devalued and perceived as risky. I learned quickly, however, that I didn't have to imagine possible scenarios, because my lived experience would demonstrate an unavoidable reality.

For years, I have waged a disorienting internal battle of assimilation where the greatest casualty has been me.

The late Dr. W. E. B. Du Bois, in his book *The Souls of Black Folk*, alluded to the concept of assimilation when he wrote about the African American dual identities of *"Blackness and Americanness,"* and the experiences of Black people as they navigate everyday life,

> *"It is a peculiar sensation, this double-consciousness, this sense of always looking at one's self through the eyes of others, of measuring one's soul by the tape of a world that looks on in amused contempt and pity. One never feels his two-ness, an American, a Negro; two souls, two thoughts, two unreconciled strivings; two warring ideals in one dark body, whose dogged strength alone keeps it from being torn asunder."[11]*

By nature and definition, the philanthropic sector is a white-dominated space. Generations of slavery, segregation, and discrimination have resulted in white people having the most access to and control over money and resources.[12] This is the environment and painful reality that professional Black fundraisers face daily, working in predominantly white spaces in the charitable sector. For fundraisers particularly, there is an expectation to assimilate, and I want to stop here and acknowledge how painful this reality is. The message we receive as Black people is, "you are not valuable, you have nothing to contribute, you cannot be here unless you give up your identity and act like us."

In Canada, the assimilation of Indigenous people was implemented as an official policy with the *Indian Act* which was explicitly designed to "Europeanize" the Indigenous population. Assimilation is also at the heart of immigration policies that strive to absorb individuals from other lands into Canadian culture and identity.[13, 14]

Assimilation is often mandated if you are in a front-facing role interacting with donors. The whiter you sound and behave, the more accepted, supported, and promoted you are by senior leaders, colleagues, and donors. The more corporate the environment, the more the pressure to assimilate. Like a carrot dangled in front of you, the reward for bending to the pressure to conform and "fit in" is the promise that career advancement is within reach, but more often than not, this is simply a devastating mirage.

In the workplace, assimilation manifests in unique ways and has acute impacts on employees.

"[For] employees who are outside the cultural mainstream, the implicit pressure to fit in may cause them to cover up stigmatized parts of their identities. The unwritten rule is that the invitation to belong is conditional as long as you fit in; this is at the cost of self-authenticity."[15]

As a Black Canadian fundraiser, most of my professional experiences have involved learning to survive in white spaces by adopting and succumbing to the pressure to conform. In these spaces, I am on guard. My Blackness is always on display in the white ocean that surrounds me. I am often the only Black fundraiser and the only person of colour on staff.

As I have moved into more senior roles, I've felt the forces of assimilation press hard against me. I've had to forfeit parts of myself in hopes of being accepted by my white colleagues. This has involved changing the way I talk, altering my actions and appearance to reflect a more "corporate/professional" appearance, all so that I could align more closely with the dominant white culture. The nonprofit workplace has been an inhospitable space for me, and many of the workplace environments I have experienced have been spaces of inherent tension. All the while, in the line of fire was my identity.

Patricia Faison, a McGill University professor, notes this pervasive pressure to conform,

> *Many Black people feel pressured to create "facades of conformity," suppressing their personal values, views, and attributes to fit in with organizational ones. But as Hewlin and her colleague Anna-Maria Broomes found in a survey of 2,226 workers in various industries and corporate settings, African Americans create these facades more frequently than other minority groups do and feel the inauthenticity more deeply. They might chemically relax (straighten) their hair, conform with coworkers' behaviour, "whitewash" their résumés by deleting ethnic-sounding names or companies, hide minority beliefs, and suppress emotions related to workplace racism.*[16]

The forces of assimilation have always been part of the Black experience. It is our slave story. Slavery and colonialism promoted the ideas of white superiority and Black inferiority (racism) throughout much of the Western world. Racist perceptions promote the view that it is more important to make others feel comfortable with us than it is to be comfortable with ourselves. Over time, the forces of assimilation have led me to develop coping strategies that often hide authentic parts of myself and downplay my racial and ethnic identity.

These pressures to assimilate frequently take the form of micro-aggressions, an everyday reality for me[17]. For example, I have suffered indirect, subtle discrimination in relation to the way I wear my natural kinky black hair and when I heat my traditional Kenyan food in the staff kitchen, experiences that have made me feel like an outsider. Tension in these situations is inevitable, because whiteness is the standard for office behaviour and my obvious Blackness is a disqualifier.

At times, I've assimilated out of fear of losing my livelihood. In those times, I have witnessed the perpetuation of inequity to protect the white power structure's status quo. Despite my effort to vacillate smoothly and inconspicuously between my authentic and conformed identities, I have been nonetheless overlooked, disregarded and passed up for promotional opportunities, as I did not "fit" into the white mold.

These repeated acts of racism have eaten away at my identity, led to self-doubt and caused me significant anxiety. My resulting exhaustion and stress have triggered workplace burnout. I struggled with who I was becoming—an inauthentic version of myself. Not the proud African woman I know that I am. These one thousand cuts have painfully led me to shift my identity between two worlds—work and home.

Less than a month ago, the executive director of the healthcare organization I worked for announced the layoffs of three women of colour, including me. The layoffs were casually communicated through a video call. The dismissing message seemed to fly in the face of the organization's mission to foster wellness and empathetic care for the vulnerable. This came as a shock to me because there was no indication to staff that layoffs were necessary. Beyond explaining that the layoffs were in response to the current COVID-19 pandemic, the executive director did not share any explanation or offer any alternative employment options. We were all recent hires to the organization and our release represented the least amount of liability for the organization. We were easy targets.

To fully explain my disbelief and shock over this decision, I need to go back several months. Seven months earlier, after being pursued and recruited by the executive director, I took a risk, leaving a secure fundraising position that I had held for three years to join this new organization. The executive director said she was growing her team and that I would be a great addition to the organization, which she was looking to diversify.

Once I started, although the organization claimed to support a diverse and inclusive working environment, I felt an immediate pressure to assimilate into the "normalcy" of the dominant culture of whiteness.

Looking back, it's now apparent that the diversity and inclusion that the executive director was seeking through hiring me was purely performative. Ultimately, however, my leadership, education and experience were expendable in the midst of a crisis, my value lost in a sea of white preference.

At the time of writing, my wound is only a few weeks old. My emotions have not all unfolded, but I want to share my reflections about this loss in real time. Finding myself laid off a matter of only months after starting this new job leaves me disenchanted and second-guessing my decision to leave my previous secure fundraising job.

I feel the economic and emotional loss of being "let go," particularly in the current environment of heightened uncertainty due to the coronavirus pandemic. I am also saddened to see another example of how Black and brown people routinely bear the brunt when organizations face difficult decisions. In the end, the decision was made to lay off three women of colour who were deemed expendable and no longer a "fit" because the organization's focus was sharply on the bottom line, where — apparently — diversity intentions cannot co-exist with the need for prudent financial management.

This organization, like many nonprofits, relies predominantly on the white community, and most of the donors are white. It is in this context that the executive director could not see a Black fundraiser's worth. I was no longer a valuable member of her team, and her diversity exercise revealed as mere tokenism. My manager's efforts to diversify the team were no longer a focus or an objective.

The loss that results from identity suppression by Black

fundraisers is two-fold. In addition to the significant personal harm done, there are also losses to the organization when Black fundraisers' unique perspectives are not shared or recognized. We bring unique experience, critical skills, and the knowledge needed to help transform the nonprofit sector and advance the causes we are championing. Equitable workplaces create a seat at the table for all to feel they belong.

Despite the pain I have endured in the profession, I choose to tell my story from a place of love and hope and possibility. Fundraising is my passion, and working in the nonprofit sector has always been my calling. I have been excluded, bullied, ignored, silenced, and marginalized doing work I was taught by my parents to love. I choose to continue working in this sector so that I can be, as Bryan Stevenson so eloquently states, "proximate" to the problems that I want to solve.

> *"You cannot be an effective problem-solver from a distance. There are details and nuances to problems that you will miss unless you are close enough to observe those details."*[18]

A Black person seeking to authentically contribute to society by serving the community finds themself contending with an onslaught of barriers built on a systemic foundation of whiteness. The result is a sense of powerlessness, mental and physical anguish. To truly combat these forces of assimilation, organizations must undo the culture that perpetuates white supremacy, causing in the process massive personal, psychological, economic, and social harm to Black employees. We must be given the space to bring our authentic selves to the workplace.

Today, I persist. I continually oppose the pain and pressure to assimilate and with each passing day, I grow more confident. With greater commitment I choose to show up in white spaces unapologetically as my true, authentic self.

►●◄

Muthoni Kariuki fell in love with nonprofits working alongside her parents. She holds an B.Sc. (Hons) from University of Toronto and a Master in Philanthropy and Nonprofit Leadership (MPNL) from Carleton University.

CHAPTER 6

Mistaking Pain for Resilience

KISHSHANA PALMER

"Pain is a temporary thing which life hardships sometimes bring. But if you trust in God and persevere the end of your pain shall soon be near."

—*Jarod "Doughboy" Trice*

I learned these words in college during a transformational period in my sophomore year. I've always had a high threshold for pain. As a child, I'd get into dust-ups and wouldn't miss a beat. As a teenager, I suffered a good old-fashioned heartbreak that made my friends cry *for* me, but I moved forward without so much as a backward glance. When I didn't get a coveted post-graduate internship and it went to one of the partners' college buddy's kids instead, I dug in and landed a role that would give me space and time to regroup. Ultimately it was the professional role that led me to a career in nonprofit management and fundraising.

Some would say *"Kishshana, that means you're resilient."*

And I would say that's true, but resiliency is often misunderstood.

A quick look at the definition for resilience reveals it as the capacity to recover quickly from difficulties. Resilience is toughness. Viewed another way, resilience is the ability of a substance or object to spring back into shape. In other words, elasticity. What does it mean to have the capacity to recover from difficult circumstances? What do you have to be made of? What do you have to withstand?

What is missing from this definition of resilience is what happens to the body, the mind and your spirit when you think about resilience, and that is…pain. Often, pain is implied but not explicitly stated. When you think about a rubber band and its ability to stretch, there is a breaking point where the rubber band starts to come away from itself and tear before it snaps and breaks.

I didn't think about pain much throughout the earliest parts of my career. I was focused, driven, on the road to the C-suite and that didn't leave much time to deliberate over what (or in many cases *who*) I allowed to hurt me. I had a goal in mind, and I was determined to make it happen. I overlooked passive-aggressive comments. I overlooked the feedback that didn't tell the whole story. I side-stepped the feelings of discomfort I experienced as I sat in meetings where decisions were being made for me and others like me, when they were harmful. I put up with it and suffered in silence.

I talked to my friends about the injustices I faced. Sometimes the phone didn't even ring twice before I was breathing down the line, "Girl, I have something to *tell* you!" I would share stories about how my CEO treated me, and would agonize over how my reaction (or lack thereof) would lead to retaliatory action of one kind or another.

Like a rubber band being stretched, I didn't notice when my capacity to snap back weakened. I didn't notice when my eye started twitching involuntarily and my neck was so tightened with knots that I looked like the hunchback of Notre Dame in the making. I didn't notice when minor colds lingered for months instead of days. I didn't slow down enough to investigate; I thought it was all part of the game. All part of the race to "the top." My body was crying out for attention. I needed a release and some rest from the daily assault on my spirit, but I kept ignoring all the signs until that (nearly) fatal day when my body *shut down…the first time*.

It started simply enough with the flu.

I figured it would be about two or three days of feeling horrible and I would bound out of bed as good as new. It *might* have happened that way, except I didn't stay in bed. I had an important meeting with a donor that I'd worked months to get, and this was just not the time to be sick. Right? So I got myself together, packed my things and got on a plane to meet this donor for one hour in another city. (You are probably wondering if I fell and bumped my head too. *And you could say that.*) What would make me get on a plane, sick and all, risking others' health to keep a meeting with a donor?

Let me explain.

Earlier in my career I'd fallen ill after a long stretch of being on the road. I had good health insurance and took a few days off to recoup. I had meetings lined up during that time and called those donors to reschedule. But when I came back to work, the CEO reassigned those donors to one of my junior team members. It didn't matter that I was working 70-80 hours a week prior to falling ill. It didn't matter that I hadn't taken a sick day in eight months even when I should have, nor did it matter that it was my right to do so. The fact that I was a C-suite team member carried little weight.

But when I came back to the office, I spoke up, and the gaslighting began. Perhaps, it was all in my head and I was making it up, imagining the reassignment and mistreatment. Then, the actions became more blatant. I found my comments unacknowledged in meetings, having some of my team go around me to get the green light on work-streams I previously said no to, and being the last to know when special events were happening. I saw that the grace extended to others — other white men and women I worked with — was rarely extended to me.

When it got to be too much to bear, I looked for another role and left the organization. It was incredibly painful to watch someone else hired after me take credit for my work. It was painful to have to sit through inter-views with prospective employers tap-dancing around why I'd left.

How could I say, "those folks were racist; there was copious amounts of cronyism and a lack of psychologi-cal safety," and still get the role? Of course I couldn't. I would practice with my recruiter friends different ways to say "that role sucked" in a way that was palatable and agreeable. I would come home from interview days in knots. And with my eye twitch never too far behind.

So, by the time my body really shut down *(the first time)*, it had been giving me warning signs for years. A simple flu turned into a nearly three-week bedridden state. Were it not for my mama and good old West Indian roots…I am not sure I'd have made it. I hadn't listened to the crying out my body was doing; I hadn't listened because the pain was disguised as resiliency.

For one, I kept getting recruited. If a role wasn't going to work out, I'd know it in eight weeks or less. Call it my "spidey" sense. And it got to a point where I didn't announce that I was even *at* a new organization until I'd been there six to eight months. Everyone wants a Black woman to come in and shake things up; be a nation builder and turn things around…in theory. In reality, this is a complete trap. There's the honeymoon period where everything you touch is novel and genius and innovative. But usually, in those first few months, especially when I needed to shake things up, the love wore thin…*and quickly*. So, moving on didn't feel as painful, and didn't sting as badly, when there was another organization waiting to scoop me up.

"Kishshana always lands."

And that is t-r-u-e. I landed the plum roles. I landed the donors. The big gifts. The big ideas. But no one—not even me—thought to stop me and ask, "what is it costing you to keep *doing this*?" This is the place where being resilient masked what was really going on with me.

Another reason I missed the cues of pain was because

I couldn't get out of the social sector. I am a skilled interviewer and landed every role I wanted and interviewed for. Except, I couldn't seem to replicate that success getting back into the corporate world. I thought re-entry to corporate life from nonprofit work would be as seamless as my exit from investment banking to fundraising had been. I even had tons of colleagues (all white and mostly women) with less experience move to foundations and to corporate social responsibility (CSR) teams at for-profit companies without so much of a speed bump.

So, I thought with all my awards, huge gifts and experience it would be straightforward for me. But no. Instead, I was *toiling* with the emotional labor of assimilation, the intense pressure of leading teams of fundraising, marketing and policy professionals, while bringing in six and seven-figure gifts with no pipeline and little support in each role. I was worn out and couldn't get out. So, I *made the best of it* and went after bigger roles at larger national nonprofit organizations, thinking if I can't get what I *really* want, I will get the best in the profession I am gifted in.

The year I finally decided to tap out was the year that the pain was too unbearable to keep putting one foot in front of the other. It was the year I realized how much I'd internalized the messages I had ingested over the course of my career. Messages that told me that I had to work harder than everyone around me, that no one would care if I wasn't there and that my contributions didn't matter. Messages that were negatively affecting me.

Finally, my body couldn't handle the assault anymore. My mind was strong, but I didn't trust anyone or have any deep relationships. I looked over my shoulder at every turn, constantly worried that I was being praised for being a star in public and torn down — *"I don't know about her"* — in private. My heart had suffered too much damage, and I could no longer manage this heartache as I had done in high school. It caught up to me, and I realized I had done major damage to myself.

That's how pain works.

If you've ever been cut or had surgery, you know that long after the wound has healed you still have the scar. It's possible to still feel pain from those scars long after they have healed. It's possible to feel pain as vivid as the day you were first cut.

If you keep the hum of pain going long enough, you don't realize when it's reached an excruciating level. You adjust to the discomfort, to the squeeze and to the searing that occurs over time. You normalize this experience until your body decides to fight back. It looks like hypertension, auto-immune diseases, chronic back pain, headaches and mental health challenges. So, if you've been taught to *keep it moving* or *don't even sweat it* and you're exhausted; it's because you have been, like me, masking your pain with your snapback (your resiliency). I encourage you to release the rubber band so it won't snap on its own.

Today, I am a work in progress.

Today, I'm relentlessly building a management and leadership company where my team feels seen, has room to innovate and take risks, and can create beautiful things in the world. I created a global community for women — a safe haven — to rest and reset as they navigate our sector and their careers. I spend my time helping Black and brown women leaders grow in their profession and find community with like-minded folks who are seeking to grow and thrive in a healthy way and build a legacy that excites them. And I have a growing pain management routine to navigate the years of professional pain I absorbed. It includes a clear faith practice, talk therapy, massage and acupuncture, time away from social media, and clear boundaries for what is and is not acceptable in my life.

I am learning to say "no" and be okay with not knowing what's going to happen on the other side of that decision. And I no longer wear my badge of resilience with honor. It's a necessary skill I honed in order to survive. Now I am polishing my thriving skills. Because I decided that pain is temporary, and perseverance means the end of my pain is near.

►●◄

Kishshana Palmer is the founder of Kishshana & Co. and of "The Rooted Collaborative" — a global learning community for Black, Indigenous and women of color leaders in the social sector.

CHAPTER 7

Perspectives of a Black Male African Fundraiser

OLUMIDE (MIDE) AKEREWUSI

Part One: The Courage to Endure

"Ignorance, allied with power, is the most ferocious enemy justice can have."

—James Baldwin[19]

Tall, Blonde, White, and preferably Male

For many Black, Indigenous and nonprofit professionals of colour, the executive team is an impenetrable fortress. Its gates are generally closed to Black people, in favour of an open-door policy to privileged white leaders and select people of other races who operate within a code. Clearly, there was an aspect of the code that I had not followed.

Wendy, our nonprofit's white, middle-class, well-meaning HR Director, stood in a small meeting room in our downtown Toronto office, addressing a team of 15 fundraisers, including myself. At this point I was serving my notice period after almost five years as Director of Leadership Philanthropy. I had helped the organisation raise $20 million of its $85-million private campaign goal. I was especially proud of this fundraising success because it also felt like a notch for Black staff, in general.

I led a small, competent team of diverse major gift fundraisers. I was also the most senior Black person in the organisation. This seemed especially strange in a charity that marketed Black and brown student success as its brand! The entire executive team was white, as was every person on the board.

Nigerian parents instill in their children, from day one, an aim for excellence expressed through enterprise and ambition. This was the case in my family, and I know it is the case for other Black cultures, people of colour, and immigrant communities, in general. This philosophy of excelling beyond the perceived norm or beyond what our white colleagues achieve is typically the mindset of people of colour. As a Black man, mediocre is not an option when working in a predominantly white environment.

Being good at my job has never been enough. I have had to also learn the *code*. The code goes like this: I have to be great at my job, great at leading a team, great at writing proposals, great at connecting with donors, and great at working with peers, board members, and the executive team. I have to be great at listening, great at public speaking, great at controlling my emotions, great at being expressive, great at keeping silent, great at showing joy, and great at hiding pain. The code will help you survive in white spaces, but it will also drain your emotional energy. On this particular day during Wendy's speech, I felt drained by a most egregious offense. But I kept the code in silence and focused on containing my pain and my shame.

That day, Wendy seemed exceptionally pleased with herself; positively delighted. She had scored a recruitment victory with her first shot at posting an executive role and brimming with excitement, she was eager to share the good news. Her description of the new recruit, a Chief Development Officer, could hardly be contained any longer. So, with child-like enthusiasm, she spilled the beans to her expectant audience. The fellow she had helped to appoint seemed like a nice chap, accomplished and ready to start his new role. Wendy described him with the kind of detail that one describes a new romantic love to their friends for the first time.

> *"And another great thing you'll like about John," she said, "He's really, really tall. He has really, really blue eyes. And blonde hair!"*

This is the nonprofit ideal — the definition and articulation of employee perfection. This is the personification of nonprofit leadership — tall, blonde, white, and preferably male. Wendy had translated an unspoken bias. She let it slip that whiteness was all along what she was looking for in the new fundraising leader. Whiteness was not a recruitment criterion on the job description; however, it was clearly important to Wendy in her selection.

As a Black male, despite my great accomplishments, I literally appear as the antithesis of the nonprofit leadership ideal. That's a pain point. No matter how hard one tries, no matter how hard one strives to achieve excellence, no matter how much one accomplishes, and no matter how well one follows the code, one simply will never be the ideal or feel a real sense of belonging. It had been made clear to me even before I tendered my resignation, that my employer would under no circumstance consider me as a worthy candidate for the Chief Development Officer role. Leadership in this organisation was white — my Blackness simply did not fit. Black leadership will always be secondary to white leadership in environments where white preservation is an unspoken rule.

An audience of witnesses, including myself, sat in silence as Wendy spoke. I do not know how others felt or even if they caught her faux pas. I generally did not discuss this moment with colleagues, I unheard what was said, and I moved on with my life.

> *Most people write me off when they see me.*
> *They do not know my story.*
> *They say I am just an African.*
> *They judge me before they get to know me.*
> *What they do not know is*
> *The pride I have in the blood that runs through my veins;*
> *The pride I have in my rich culture and the history of my people;*
> *The pride I have in my strong family ties and the deep connection to my community;*
> *The pride I have in the African music, African art, and African dance;*

The pride I have in my name and the meaning behind it.
Just as my name has meaning, I too will live my life with
meaning.
So you think I am nothing?
Don't worry about what I am now,
For what I will be, I am gradually becoming.
I will raise my head high wherever I go
Because of my African pride,
And nobody will take that away from me.

— Idowu Koyenikan[20]

Afro-phobic Leaders in "Africa-saving" Charities

The nonprofit sector's most incredible and worrying irony is that "Africa-saving" charities working in the field of international development are among the whitest of all the nonprofit branches. They are as exclusionary of Black leadership as are for example the ballet, opera, and hockey organisations, and sometimes even more so. In fact, international development organisations maintain brand prestige by eschewing African leadership. Their boards and executive teams are strongholds that reflect Afro-phobic culture among white leaders and white donors.

Pete was a white, middle-aged, middle-class, Chief Executive Officer at one of Canada's leading youth-serving international development agencies. As he invited me into his office to take a seat, I was, as I always am at the job interview stage, on high alert. Even before I could enact the code, I sensed something was up. I was, after all, an African in an international development organisation that depicts Africans as hungry, poor,

AIDS/HIV suffering, needy Blacks, waiting to be saved by the good and generous white people.

I realize international development agencies' co-optation of my African brand and that of Africa's diaspora. These agencies depict imagery and language that crystalize opinions among the general white public about what it means to be African. My own middle-class privileged status is no competition for the millions of grotesque, dehumanizing images we have all seen of flies circling a young African child, dead African bodies, or bare-breasted African mothers begging for food. It's no wonder that some years back, I found myself at pains to convince a well-meaning acquaintance that the majority of Africans do indeed live in houses and generally speaking, not in huts. This person's understanding of Africanness was entirely formed by the perceptions that development organisations had created in his mind. It is what novelist Chimamanda Ngozi Adichie calls the *"Single Story"*—a one-sided, prejudicial view based on stereotypes rather than a balanced understanding.

This one-sided view is, in my experience, prevalent in international development agencies. Such single stories are inevitable in exclusively-white leadership environments because so few of them recruit African leaders to tip the balance of systemic mis-education.

Pete had never met me. He had only heard about me through my friend Stephanie. She was the Chief Development Officer at the organisation Pete led, and was close to expecting her child. She was looking for a person to cover her role during her absence and called me a few weeks before her maternity leave. I felt pleased and proud that Stephanie had placed the call to me, and I agreed to meet her team and Pete to essentially clinch the deal on the day this incident occurred.

Stephanie's team seemed nervous when they met me. They were polite but perhaps unsure about me. Some seemed doubtful that a Black man was qualified for the role, though by now I was 15 years into a distinguished international fundraising career, crafted in two philanthropic continents, working with some of the world's largest charities and global philanthropists. I had just completed a nearly three-year term as Chief Development Officer at a global community charity, where I established that organisation's first professional fundraising team and weathered the 2008 recession while overseeing growth in revenue. I was also new to Canada. A *"newcomer"* as Canadians put it and an *"outsider"* as my then colleagues had ominously described me.

While some of Stephanie's team were polite, I sensed hostility from others and tried to deploy the code to allay their inherent fears about impending Black leadership. One thing about being a Black leader is that your credentials always need to be proven. No matter how stellar you are or how extensive your track record is, Black people have to prove over and over again that they really are the professionals that their CVs and reputations say that they are. As the actor Gabrielle Union so eloquently states in her book, *We're Going to Need More Wine*, being a Black person is about understanding *"what it is to be automatically infantilized and have it be assumed that you don't have the talent or the skill set required to do your job."* It's like having a 25-year membership at an exclusive club, and yet the same receptionist insists on seeing your identification whenever you enter the establishment.

Stephanie's team asked some deep, probing questions and I provided knowledgeable answers. Some seemed more at ease after they got to know me during our one-hour meeting. Pete was the final hurdle that day. His impression, his power, his decision, and his waving of a thumb up or down would decide if the temporary role would be mine.

Pete's office was moderately decorated, a fairly typical arrangement with a desk, chairs, and a round table. Maps and pictures of African people adorned his walls and several magazines and books were dispersed across his office space. I remember how bright the day was when I entered Pete's office. It was a crisp, cold day. As I entered, upon his invitation, he was seated with his back to me.

His desk was facing a window that overlooked a North Toronto high-street. It added to the impression of his power, the way being on the 50th floor in an office building overlooking Wall Street must feel. Pete took a moment to complete what he was typing at his desk. He swiveled in his chair gracefully to face me.

He was seeing me for the first time. I stood, waiting to be invited to take a seat. He took a handful of seconds to scan me, pausing as he contemplated my 6 ft 4 in African male frame. Our eyes locked — the silence continued for a few more seconds, allowing Pete to offer his troubling confession, *"You know, Mide, I am very nervous about recruiting to this role."*

Pete was clearly not enamoured with me. It wasn't anything I said or I did. He instantly disliked who he saw. All of my accomplishments and accolades, hard work and drive; all of my skills and knowledge, my versatility, and craft; all of my education and my training, my understanding of global issues, and leadership experience at several large international organisations. None of it mattered to Pete at that very moment. He was on high alert — he decided within the first five seconds of seeing me that I was not the person for this job. I had no place and would not belong in his organisation during his leadership, not temporarily. Not ever.

Now what? Pete had let his racism do the talking but he was mindful enough to catch himself and to mince his words. He had respectfully omitted the word "you." However, I had heard the unspoken loud and clear. My interpretation of the situation then and now is that his thoughts echoed the following: *"You know, Mide, I am very nervous about recruiting YOU to this role."*

Perhaps Pete feared African leadership. Perhaps it was offensive to him that a Black man would occupy a role in his "Africa-saving," white-led organisation. Even though Pete's organisation was established to serve African children with health, aid, and social welfare, it appeared to be custom to exclude people of African descent from taking leadership positions in donor countries such as Canada, the USA, the UK, and parts of Europe. Nowhere else is an anti-Black leadership environment more prevalent than in the world's favourite white-led development organisations.

Stephanie called to tell me the news. I, of course, already knew the result seconds into my meeting with Pete. She sounded slightly apprehensive over the phone, perhaps even embarrassed. She told me that Pete had called a friend and former colleague from his previous youth-serving international development organisation. This white colleague had not been part of the recruitment process, and had far less fundraising experience than I, according to Stephanie. However, Pete obviously felt more comfortable appointing a white friend out of the blue. Of course he did! Friends appointing friends has been the gold standard of nonprofit leadership recruitment for decades. This is how organisations stay white at the very top.

Sometime after returning from maternity leave, Stephanie (a blonde and blue-eyed Chief Development Officer) left Pete's organisation. Her replacement was blonde and blue-eyed Charlotte. The interesting fact about Charlotte was that I had recruited her as a VP on my team while I was Chief Development Officer in another organisation. As a fundraiser and executive, I was also vastly more experienced than Charlotte.

Here's where the pain sits: It's less about being rejected for a job; people of all races must endure the disappointment of job rejection. The pain is in the knowledge that my Blackness is reason enough to be rejected for a job, irrespective of my talent and skill. Another pain stems from the fact that, unfortunately, there are hundreds of Petes in leadership roles across the nonprofit sector, leading our best-known organisations. They tout civil rights and racial equality yet practice the most destructive form of racism—the racism hidden behind a veneer of help and support for Black people.

Although these are my painful stories from the past,

they are also the stories of Black people in the nonprofit sector today. However, they needn't be the painful stories of the future. I believe we can, with courage, build a movement to challenge systemic anti-Black racism in the nonprofit sector. Our actions will need to be consistent and continuous, just as racism itself is continuous and consistent.

Part Two: The Courage to Take Action

"We are not fighting for integration, nor are we fighting for separation. We are fighting for recognition as human beings...In fact, we are actually fighting for rights that are even greater than civil rights and that is human rights."

—Malcolm X [21]

∞

Race and Whiteness in the Nonprofit Sector

Throughout my career, just as I have valued Black people and people of colour, I have cherished my relationships with white people, colleagues, peers, team members, managers, friends, associates, clients and mentors. As an immigrant to Canada, I am proud that my personal and professional network has grown to be as culturally rich and diverse as the City of Toronto itself. We have all at times in our lives required love and friendship, and wise counsel and support; for me that has come from people of all races, including white people.

When I write or speak about white people, I do not

speak in terms of the colour of one's skin. I speak in terms of people who share a specific politicized philosophy that their "whiteness" affords them — a certain power of authority over people like me who have darker skin, and in particular, are African. It's also important to note that I have endured situations in which darker-skinned people have deployed "whiteness" to inflict pain on me or to undermine me.

I have only ever had one non-white supervisor in my career. Within a white power structure, his attitude towards me was as oppressive as any I have experienced. His first act as a new CEO was to remove me from the executive team, banish me from the C-suite, and replace me with a white female whom he apparently perceived to be less "challenging" to work with. Though he and I shared a similar skin tone, his mindset in our predominantly white working environment was white. To be clear, whiteness can exist within the mindset of people with darker skin — it's called internalised oppression.

The Alberta Civil Liberties Research Centre's stance, through a series of excerpts from thought leaders, most powerfully emphasizes my point. I take the liberty of sharing their ideas to elaborate on a perspective I also share:[22]

As with the term "race," it is important to clarify the differences between "white" (a category of "race" with no biological or scientific foundation) and "whiteness" as a powerful social construction with very real, tangible, violent effects. Here are some useful definitions of whiteness, followed by a list of its key features:

Racism is based on the concept of whiteness—a powerful fiction enforced by power and violence. Whiteness is a constantly shifting boundary separating those who are entitled to have certain privileges from those whose exploitation and vulnerability to violence is justified by their not being white.[23]

'Whiteness', like 'colour' and 'Blackness,' are essentially social constructs applied to human beings rather than veritable truths that have universal validity. The power of whiteness, however, is manifested by the ways in which racialized whiteness becomes transformed into social, political, economic, and cultural behaviour. White culture, norms, and values in all these areas become normative natural. They become the standard against which all other cultures, groups, and individuals are measured and usually found to be inferior.[24]

Drawing on Ruth Frankenberg's seminal work on white childhood, feminism, and racism, the authors of *Teach Me to Thunder: A Manual for Anti-Racism Trainers*, write that whiteness is:

a dominant cultural space with enormous political significance, with the purpose to keep others on the margin...white people are not required to explain to others how 'white' culture works because 'white' culture is the dominant culture that sets the norms. Everybody else is then compared to that norm...In times of perceived threat, the normative group may well attempt to reassert its normativity by asserting elements of its cultural practice more explicitly and exclusively.[25]

Waking Up to Race and Racism

The difference between racism in the UK, where I was born and raised, and racism in Canada, where I have lived for the last 12 years, is that in the UK, racists tend not to hide. They are open and often proud of their bigotry, and are generally accepted, if not celebrated within the most public of circles — political parties, news media, publishing, and even the entertainment and sports industries. In Canada, on the other hand, racism publicly appears as an affront to the Canadian value of fairness and is therefore intentionally minimised as a fringe issue rather than a systemic problem.

My sense of racism in the workplace, both in the UK and in Canada, was always heightened when I sought promotion in recognition of my accomplishments within a team. Despite consistently being the relationship fundraiser who was raising the most funds among my peers, I was regularly denied the opportunity to climb the career ladder. For a 14-year stretch, while I worked for five large, white-led nonprofits, a discussion about career progression resulted in three supervisors in three organisations obstructing my career progress. I have also endured demotion twice, despite exceptional performance. These experiences all led to my subsequent resignation. In my case, this fact becomes a racism issue not because I was denied opportunities at promotion, but because on each of the four occasions, a far less experienced and less accomplished white fundraiser was offered the role by the same supervisor who obstructed my promotion.

Advancing through the ranks of a nonprofit organisation happens to be a rarity for talented Black employees. This is clearly evidenced by the fact that so few white-led organisations can boast of Black presence on their executive teams.

For much of my 25 years in the sector, I have quietly whispered the effects of racism on my own well-being to trusted Black friends and people of colour, while always following the code in my relationships with white colleagues. This is no doubt because I have always worked in white environments where challenging whiteness is a 'Career Limiting Move' (CLM). However, ironically, it is also true to say that simply being Black is a CLM in the nonprofit sector.

Despite the growing vocal objections of Black people to racism in the nonprofit sector, only a small minority of well-intentioned white allies are prepared to do anything in their power about it. The most silent group are white men. Very seldom have I encountered a vocal white male activist for Black people in the nonprofit sector. This speaks to a broader complicity and to the reward for whiteness.

This gender distinction is important because although the majority of the Canadian nonprofit sector's roles are occupied by women, men still occupy most of the executive roles and board positions. The disproportionate power that white men yield can and should be directed towards outrage at decades of institutionalised racism in the sector. However, the silence and subsequent inaction of the majority of white male executives and board members lead to silence and inaction across many white-led organisations.

Martin Luther King Jr. put our current situation aptly,

"In the end, we will remember not the words of our enemies, but the silence of our friends."

Perhaps, some white people feel they have nothing to gain and everything to lose by demonstrating outrage to the point of action on behalf of or with their Black peers and colleagues. Voicing concern at often-hidden, systemic, anti-Black practices is after all a daunting task. I must confess, that as a Black man, I was conditioned to be polite about racism in the workplace for more than two decades, even though I experienced racism every day. It became, in my mind, an offence to the code to openly acknowledge my own oppression. It was far easier to put my head down and get on with my job than to challenge the racists, and for years I refused to speak about it. I even developed a mantra, "I am not the diversity guy. I am the fundraising guy." Whiteness has the effect of rendering silence and inaction in all but the most courageous.

However, we all must become courageous activists in defeating systemic anti-Black racism. Black and white colleagues and the brave actions of Black women in the nonprofit sector have led me to finally speak out about racism in this way at this point. Namely, I credit my sister-friend, Nneka Allen, for showing me how to challenge the white power structure in the nonprofit world.

A major motivation for me taking action is the realisation that nothing will ever change if we commit to silence instead of action. Change is needed if our next generation of Black leaders is to remain in the sector and contribute to its future sustainability.

The writer Ta-Nehisi Coates speaks about the problem of racism as one where white people often refuse to believe that they are its perpetrators. We fight an enemy that is present and real in our lives but invisible, fake, and deniable in the eyes of our white colleagues. This makes navigating racism a full-time job for Black people, alongside our substantive roles as employees, consultants, volunteers and donors in the nonprofit sector.

The most common response to a complaint about racism is a declaration of inertia—a "not knowing" of what to do when Black people express their oppression. At its extreme, this "not knowing" predictably results in CLM penalties for Black people who raise the complaint—disbelief, minimisation, loss of one's employment, ostracism, exclusion, ridicule, bullying, gossiping, and treatment that reinforces the very exclusion which Black people spotlight. This often serves as a contradiction to the offer of allyship pronounced by white colleagues. True allyship involves waking-up, speaking out and taking action against systemic anti-Black racism in support of Black nonprofit organisation employees, consultants, volunteers, and donors.

Equity as a Solution to Systemic Anti-Black Racism

Lately, some white-led nonprofit organisations have acknowledged their role in facilitating and are now challenging systemic anti-Black racism in a sector that has, for all intents and purposes, become anti-Black, Afro-phobic, and racist. While performative promises and statements of change are commendable, such statements continue to place Black people at the periphery of white acceptability as opposed to in positions of control within the discussion. As is said in the disability activist movement — *"Nothing for us, without us."* We cannot establish an equitable nonprofit sector if power is not shared, harnessed or even transferred to Black people at the stage of idea inception.

Equity is the result of people exercising choice, voice, and control over their own lives for the collective good. It involves systems that guarantee fair access to money and power among all people. Equity transcends barriers established to exclude people on the basis of race, culture, colour, religion, gender, sexuality, ability, age, wealth, and immigration status.[26] Equity is also a barometer for how a society expresses its human values and responsibilities towards others. It is essential that equity is at the heart of every functioning nonprofit organisation's mission, as well as being the driver for those who grant funds. Without equity, an organisation's mission, vision, and values will fail.

Dealing with Pain—Looking to the future

In my first three years of becoming a professional fundraiser, I was promoted three times, but never again experienced job promotion for the next 17 years of my career as a nonprofit employee. As I consider the alchemy of how I forged my career, in those first three years, I give credit to white supervisors who were skilled in their jobs and generous in sharing their knowledge with me. I give credit to supervisors who offered to invest in my training and encouraged me to improve and enhance my abilities. Most of all, these supervisors saw my talent as well as my Blackness. However, my Blackness for them was not a threat but rather an asset to their own pursuit of equity within the team and to the organisation we served. I had a perspective that was different from theirs, and they valued my opinions and encouraged me to be expressive. As our team's success grew, they did all in their power to advance my career with love and support.

Thereafter most of the advancements in my career came not from having caring supervisors who helped me navigate promotion but from white supervisors who eventually forced my resignations through incidents where racism became a catalyst for me to resign from my job. I have neither the time nor the space to include the full stories of two white male supervisors whose egos were intimidated not just by my skin colour and height but also by the fact that I would not succumb to their attempts to bully or control me. My response was to stand my ground and be unequivocal about the values and standards that I apply to working relationships — respect is one value that I am uncompromising about. I eventually resigned from both positions.

Neither is there time or space to pen a story about the recruiting manager who refused to grant me a permanent role despite me raising the organisation's largest major gift, equivalent to $6.5 million at the time. I immediately ended my contract and landed my first substantive professional fundraising role.

Lastly, I wish there was an opportunity to share more about a discussion with a well-known Canadian socialite who agreed to make a donation to a project I presented to her. She had a stipulation: *"not a single dollar"* of her philanthropic gift should be used to support the youth of the Islamic faith. I informed her that I would not accept her donation with such a stipulation, and she ended up making her donation without the stipulation.

When it comes to personally dealing with the pain of systemic anti-Black racism, I have first had to develop an internalised emotional mechanism for dealing with the shock. A racist act usually occurs on the most mundane of days and most routine of tasks, and typically it happens so quickly that the memory of it is often the most tangible of what remains.

For me, the most painful racist experiences in the workplace also serve as the most disorienting attempts to try and undermine my humanity. I use much of my energy to immediately stabilise my thoughts and continue with the task at hand. To dwell on racist experiences just exacerbates my pain, but a problem ignored, never quite disappears. The daily occurrences of racism through micro-aggressions and blatant xenophobia also require pragmatic solutions, which for me include:

1. Being clear about my passion and purpose, and reminding myself about why I joined the nonprofit sector: to build a career out of the pursuit of equity.

2. Referring to my network of trusted colleagues who share different perspectives and provide wise counsel during the most stressful times.

3. Volunteering in projects where I can use the skills that have often been prohibited in the workplace — for example, independent decision-making. When racist barriers are built in the workplace, a voluntary project can serve as an outlet for rebuilding self-belief.

These are not comprehensive suggestions for dealing with systemic anti-Black racism; they are simply my most rewarding coping mechanisms. However, beyond my individualised coping mechanisms, my fear still exists.

When I consider my greatest fear for the future of our nonprofit sector, it is that charities will grow to be irrelevant and thereby unsustainable in our society because they ultimately fail in their duty to deliver equity. We already know that there have been years of decline in the number of people giving to registered charities[27], and that donor trust and confidence in the nonprofit sector is already extremely low.[28] The ongoing reports of cronyism between a leading charity and the Canadian government, the accusations of sexual exploitation within the international development movement, the exclusion of Black-led nonprofit organisations within private philanthropy, and the stories of racism we now hear every day demonstrate that radical change is required in the nonprofit sector.

My fear, however, is balanced with the hope that if we consistently challenge the systems of anti-Black racism, we will be able to more effectively challenge all other forms of exclusion, unfairness, and discrimination in the sector. This current conscious moment that is geared towards the important debate about systemic anti-Black racism is ideal to explore collective considerations for tackling racism. Together, I hope we can pursue the important steps of action that are required, for ourselves, for others, and for our future.

▸●◂

Olumide (Mide) Akerewusi, Founder and CEO of AgentsC Inc, holds a B.Sc. (Hons) degree in Business Studies and Sociology from the University of Surrey, and an M.Sc. (Econ) in the Political Economy of Asia and Africa from SOAS, University of London. He serves on the Board of 100 Strong.

FREEDOM

CHAPTER 8

Unlocking My Authentic Voice, A Journey to Liberating and Defining Myself

NIAMBI MARTIN-JOHN

"Whatever we believe about ourselves and our ability comes true for us."

—*Susan L Taylor* [29]

Everyone has a story. The sharing and retelling of those stories, and snippets of our life experiences is what enables us to relate to others and binds us together as human beings. When we tell our stories, I believe that the shape of our recollections is influenced by the audience with whom we are sharing. Often, we make accommodations for the listener so that we can manage their perceptions of whom we want to be in their eyes. At times, those reconstructions can be beneficial to propel us to find more depth within ourselves — to find a type of freedom. But there are times when we are forced to edit our stories, and by extension ourselves, to make space for the fragility of others, to free others from ancestral guilt, or to imbue a false sense of allyship that hasn't really been earned.

Throughout our lives, we may straddle that place between wanting to tell our stories in our authentic voices and restricting our voices to navigate more easily through the complexities of a society, much of which is unready and often unwilling to hear us. However, I believe the potency of our stories dies a little each time we tell an apocryphal version of our reality. Owning the voice in which we tell our stories and discovering the freedom to do so forcefully and fearlessly, propels us forward unimpeded and empowered — giving rise to greater self-awareness, stronger resolve and increased clarity that once activated, only serves to generate more stories of activism, change and courage.

In our personal lives, finding the resolve to separate or weed out relationships that require us to 'edit' ourselves can seem less daunting. But in professional settings, we carry a burden of compliance that often compels us to present our stories in the most inauthentic ways.

For years, as I struggled to build a career in fundraising, I felt compelled to compartmentalize my experiences, taking into the workplace only those things that would not threaten, challenge or upset the status quo. This meant that I worked overtime to fit a mold, one that I did not create, contribute to, or identify with. I had to conform in order to be accepted, seen and validated. What occurred to me as I did this complex dance is that my white peers felt no such obligation. They moved in the workplace with an ease, something I interpreted as an air of arrogance and fearlessness that I would never dare to take on. Over the years, as I shared this observation with Black peers, many confirmed what I now call the 'white exemption clause'.

You see, the historical socialization of my white peers in the North American context affords them great power and privileges, including an affirmation that all spaces were created for them. They have permission to not only take up space but to make space for themselves in a way that I simply never could. This type of grooming nurtures and feeds the feeling of superiority and ownership of the process and structure that builds up systemic barriers against Black people. Repeatedly throughout my journey, this issue has emerged.

When I moved to Canada more than 20 years ago, I had no road map or frame of reference for the things that would eventually shape my thoughts about the Black experience or my professional life. Growing up in Dominica, my Blackness was a construct closely tied to my cultural identity rather than my ethnicity. There we immersed ourselves in the celebration of our food, music, art and language, all of which are heavily influenced by African, European and Native culture. There it was the commonality of our experiences as one people that took precedence, and not our race. Therefore, even though I was keenly aware and proud of my Blackness, my race, in Dominica, did not affect the quality of my life, access or achievements. Almost everyone looked like me, and even those who didn't have a kinship with us had a deference to Pan-Africanism that transcended racial identity. I never had to declare my race on a form for school, to receive medical attention, or on a community survey. I never had to apologize for my Blackness so that someone could feel comfortable in my presence.

In Canada, I quickly had to reevaluate what being Black meant—who did people see when I walked into a room, and what level of potential did they ascribe to me based on their preconceptions? For a time, I felt powerless to influence the trajectory of my life in this new country, and the temptation to surround myself with familiar things was very strong. The employment rejection letters, unanswered applications in the hundreds, passive-aggressive recruiters and micro-aggressions — *"Where are you from?," "Is that an accent I hear?"*—made me move with a caution that I was unaccustomed to. But as is the case with other immigrants, I didn't come here to fail. The person that my family and friends knew was strong and confident was definitely not one to move timidly. With this in mind, I forged ahead and into my first job as a receptionist secured through an agency. The job lasted exactly one week.

After my first week, the owner of the company contacted Human Resources with instructions telling the agency that I was no longer needed because he could not understand my accent. He said that neither he nor his customers were able to understand me. This was my first time learning about my "otherness" in a context that did not empower me, but instead had devastated me in ways that I still struggle to describe. This man had not even met me and had exchanged no more than ten words with me, yet he decided that he did not like my accent and I therefore was not welcomed to work in his company.

Some say that every disappointment is a set up for something greater. This has been my experience, and I believe it in the fibre of my being. After I picked myself up from that hurtful exchange, I determined I would not let the pain stop me. I decided to volunteer (eventually landing a paid position), within an area that I felt at the time would be more inclusive and diverse—the arts.

This position led to my first real job in fundraising and an understanding of philanthropy from a lens that was foreign to me. Most of my previous exposure to philanthropy was through the work of foreign aid and relief agencies in the third world. It was through this job that I learned about the intricacies and complexities of fundraising. I soaked up everything I could like a sponge, while being keenly aware that I was earning far less than my peers. I remember appealing to the company president on more than one occasion requesting that my compensation be reviewed, only to be reminded that I did not have any previous Canadian experience. They were quick to remind me that I was learning a lot in my role. Again, the power dynamic here was considerable. They wanted me to be grateful and quiet.

I often found myself measuring the benefits of speaking out against the grossly inappropriate and discriminatory behaviour versus building a sustainable career. I had not yet found my voice or the freedom to be unafraid and bold to challenge powerful systems and people who were committed to my disadvantage. I did retain my resolve to do my job well and channeled those same negative experiences into being more empathetic, a great listener and a strong closer — essential skills for every fundraiser's toolkit. Reflecting on the role that launched my career, I realize that it was here I first experienced the 'white exemption clause' which simply was, *"the rules do not apply to everyone in the organization."*

In this first development role, I hired and trained fundraising managers across North America to execute campaigns on behalf of various clients. One of my responsibilities was to present to all our new employees as part of the on-boarding process employment contracts that included, among other expectations, a non-compete clause. From time to time there were people who signed only reluctantly after long explanations of various parts of the contract. On one memorable day, while I was dealing with an older white male and prospective employee, he explained to me that not only was he not going to sign the contract, but also that no Black, immigrant b*#ch could get him to do it, either!

Recalling the encounter now, I can reduce it to a ten-second story, but in the moment, it felt like time had frozen. I simply wasn't equipped to address his direct derogatory reference to my race and gender or what I assume was his disdain for my presence in Canada. I shared his response with the senior leaders and Human Resources but to add insult to injury, this person was allowed to proceed with his employment, in an obvious breach of the organization's code of conduct. Instead, he was reassigned to work with someone else, as if I had triggered him in some way. I wondered to myself whether I could get away with similar behaviour and knew without asking the answer was absolutely not.

The thing about experiencing racism or discrimination is that every encounter should help you shape a new weapon for your personal defense and response. The first few racial traumas may catch you by surprise and leave you speechless. You may even talk yourself into believing that what you experienced wasn't really racist. However, as you accumulate more experiences, it becomes more obvious and unquestionable. To counterbalance the racial trauma and diminish the ferocity of those interactions, I had to establish my voice. I now carry with me a quote from Mary McLeod Bethune, Civil Rights Activist, Philanthropist and Educator. She states:

"If we accept and acquiesce in the face of discrimination, we accept the responsibility ourselves and allow those responsible to salve their conscience by believing that they have our acceptance and concurrence. We should, therefore, protest openly everything that smacks of discrimination or slander."

In the years that followed, and as my career began to progress and I landed more senior leadership roles, I found myself increasingly challenged even by those who had hired me. I saw myself in positions where I had to justify my every move even while outperforming my peers. I experienced one particularly brutal work culture with such a hostile environment that my creativity and personality were suppressed to such an extent that I could not do my job. It was here that a senior person to whom my boss reported personally approached me to tell me I was a lousy writer despite my strong writing reputation. I can laugh now, but at the time, that feedback, from someone who knew me only a couple of weeks and who had not seen any of my original work, gave me pause.

Not, however, for long. Because I quickly realized she could not break my spirit. I had already experienced this type of unfounded dismissal too many times and had long before determined that any devaluation of my work was not reflective of the truth. I decided that my way forward was to continue to perform, with excellence as always.

There is a common misconception (among white people) that the type of work we do in the charitable sector is work best suited for white people. Too often, I carried the label of being aggressive, *"why are you so angry, why are you yelling,"* even as the real aggressors retreated to the safety of the "white exemption clause." Daring to stand up for myself, being direct and simply not accepting unjust treatment earned me a reputation of being "tough," but ignored that I am collaborative, empathetic and willing to mentor and invest in staff in a way that is rare.

Most organizations in the social sector are devoted to improving the lives of people, whether by creating access, funding cures and interventions for diseases or addressing the needs of under-served communities. The result is an assumption that most employees' personal values align with the organization's mission. The ugly truth, however, is that for most people of colour, the sector is not a safe place. The challenges that we face at the hands of our white peers directly contradicts the image the sector would like to uphold.

To persevere despite the obstacles placed in my way was not easy. And I couldn't do it alone. I knew that to change the trajectory of my career, I needed help from people who would help amplify my voice and open doors. Starting the process of building my support system required deep introspection, a suspension of my ego and careful evaluation about how sponsorship could help me in the work environment. I proceeded to build my network with leaders who saw the value of my work and understood the vision and passion that I offered.

This included gathering a network of white leaders who were willing to, even temporarily, suspend judgement and honestly see the value of my contributions and invest their time in petitioning others to make space for me. In many instances, I couldn't navigate new opportunities without these sponsors because the system is structured so that the validity of my experience and my broad acceptance would never gain traction unless marketed by white people to white people.

As a Black person these relationships can be extremely frustrating because the system is set up to reinforce the white saviour complex. If white people have to repeatedly tell your story you begin to lose ownership of that story. Even though sponsorship suggests that one is supporting you with no expectation of personal reward in return, it has been my experience that some of the people who helped me progress in my career required my deep gratitude for the favour they did for me. I know with certainty that many times those same people knew my skills and abilities would further their personal and professional agenda. It was in these instances when the return 'favours' would be expected.

There were times when the idea of me in a senior position seemed hard for some to accept, with one co-worker asking me on the eve of a promotion, "Do you think you are being promoted just so that the organization can have a Black person in a senior role?"

A real and crippling result of being a Black person on a senior leadership team is that we are often given a nice tidy box along with our promotions. As long as we stay inside that package of assigned and ascribed behaviours and expectations — saying yes, turning a blind eye to discriminatory behaviour, ignoring inflammatory comments, smiling when someone says or does something that is covertly and even overtly racist so that we can all pretend to be comfortably getting along—all remains well.

However, deciding to imprint your story and build your legacy outside the lines of your portfolio and therefore outside your assigned box can have dire consequences. Like many before me, I have been fired, laid off, demoted, and blackballed for speaking truth, standing up and demanding better. No one will actually tell you why the budget for your role suddenly dried up, or why the restructuring doesn't include you even if they had gone through great pains to let you know how much you were respected and valued in the past. You have to know ahead of time that the consequence of standing up

often does not lead to victory in the way that you antici-
pate — a promotion or being seen as a champion. No, it
may very well be the end of the road in an organization,
group or association.

But there is freedom in raising your voice.

I have reached that point in my career where I am
willing to face the consequences, and I think you will
find that many Black people with any measure of success
in the sector, had to reach the point where being let go
or being the outsider was something they were willing
to accept in return for owning their story.

One of my most recent encounters was with a senior
leader in my organization. He called me into his office
for a chat. He wanted to let me know what an integral
part of the organization I was. How my contributions
were exceptional, and how much I had taught him about
fundraising. He told me that he respected me and that
I was one of the smartest people he knew. And then the
other shoe dropped, *"However, I am going to need you to
tone down your 'smarts'"* he said. *"It makes it difficult for me
to keep everyone happy if you are intimidating your peers by
knowing and sharing ideas about how they should do their
jobs. Could you just not share so much of what you know?"*

Unlike the first time I had experienced this type of
deliberate and calculated silencing of my voice, I now had
a well-stocked toolkit to help me navigate the conversation. I had become accustomed to being told how excellent my work was only to be treated in the opposite
way by my superiors. I was used to being drained of my
intellectual power to ensure that others above me looked
great while receiving no credit for my contributions.

This time, however, something in me decided this was not going to happen again. What the senior leader was describing as my intimidation of my peers for being "too smart" was, in fact, me creating and taking space for myself. I challenged him to clarify his words by asking if he was requesting that I dumb myself down so that others could feel better about themselves, and less insecure about their lack of knowledge. I then asked him further whether I would have been checked like this if I were a white man or woman?

All around this organization, white men were being celebrated, climbing the professional ladder at alarming rates, while I am told to dumb down my knowledge! It was Shirley Chisholm who said, *"If they don't give you a seat at the table, bring a folding chair."* So here I was, folding chair in hand, taking a seat at a table to which I was reluctantly being accommodated.

I can tell you that no matter how deliberate the actions of your oppressor, they are *never* prepared for you to fight back. They are accustomed to going unchallenged and getting away with bad behaviour. When I challenged this obviously sexist and racist feedback, he immediately backtracked, reminding me that he had complimented me several times during the conversation. He told me how valuable I was to him and to the organization.

It is such a mind trick when this dynamic exists between you and someone who has the power to take your job from you. Do you appease them by pretending to have misunderstood what their real intent was? Or do you stand your ground and force them to admit that they acted poorly?

These are the choices that we must make on a daily basis. Every day, we must decide whether we will be true to ourselves or toe the line so that we can keep our jobs or a work environment peaceful. In my case, I chose to challenge the behaviour when it happened, whether directed at me or others, until it became clear that I was not allowing any incidents of racism, bullying, denigrating speech or actions.

It got to a point where work became a chore. While working overtime to maintain the outward face of unity, and to keep my own team motivated and productive, I was no longer enjoying any interactions with my superiors. It became a burden and took its toll on my physical and mental health. And, finally, when it was clear that things would not improve, I decided to leave the organization.

I had written my resignation letter a hundred times in my head, and when the day came to hand it in, I experienced such a feeling of joy, relief and freedom. I knew that I had taken a bold step, one that would more than likely mean losing friends and allies. But it was a necessary step, a message to the organization that if they continued to mistreat and disregard their employees, they would lose some of their strongest and most productive staff.

I, however, was prioritizing *me*. After speaking with Human Resources, I approached my direct supervisor to let her know that I was resigning. And I wasn't surprised by her reaction. She didn't inquire about what had led me to abandon a role and a team that I had devoted so many years to building. And even though I had previously provided her with feedback about how her lack of leadership, follow-through and support was negatively impacting my work, she did not take any responsibility. There was no personal introspection on her part.

Her response was to tell me she had observed that I hadn't been happy for some time now anyway. But less than ten minutes later, after I had returned to my desk, she approached me asking me for another one-on-one in her office where she told me she would have to hire three people to replace me. That was a bold admission on her part. She knew that I had been working at a pace that was far above my peers. She knew that my contribution was superior and yet she had shown so little appreciation and acknowledgement for my work. I had made the right decision. I was glad to leave.

Working in this sector, I am used to being the only person of colour in a room. In the last few years, however, I have seen more Black people enter the sector, and with that, key leaders and professional associations have started to take note. But there seems to be a decided fear among those in positions of power that we may mobilize.

In one organization I worked, any gathering of Black women caused raised eyebrows — what are you guys plotting? Us Black women would jokingly refer to our social connections as the *"where two or more are gathered"* group because of the strong perception of us gathering in any capacity, meant that we must be planning a revolt. But of course, our white peers were free to gather in large groups, whenever they wanted and as they pleased without comment. In defiance of this, we chose to define ourselves as mentors, friends and empowering partners while also being agitators and change agents choosing to take back the power and characterize ourselves on our own terms.

Black people are indeed gathering and creating networks of support. The fear that such a coming together will upset the imbalance of things and actually challenge the sector to see Black people as competent, capable and worthy of leadership and power is palpable.

As more of us step forward to help shape the sector, some are transitioning out of it, exhausted from the work of either constantly proving yourself to retain roles, or being excluded from roles that we are more than qualified to have. This exodus, though, is cause to build a foundation of support, particularly for Black women who are creating a safe space reinforced by the commonalities of our collective stories.

I had to learn that no one could free me from the cycle of checking myself at the door when I went to work, softening my accent, adjusting my tone, suppressing my creativity, suffocating my Blackness — I had to find my power and stand resolute ready to face whatever came with claiming freedom of self. So I implemented a few rules that helped me to rid myself of the weight of conformity.

First, I gave myself the permission to say "no."

If I don't feel comfortable doing something, or if I'm feeling maxed out, I say no. I also learned to determine when my "no" requires me to give an explanation, and when "no" is simply enough. Someone once asked me to convey a message to an internal stakeholder in a way that I felt was unnecessarily aggressive and did not preserve the dignity of that person. I declined to do so. If this was the only way the message could be conveyed, then I knew I was the wrong person for the job.

Second, I learned to take credit for my work and my contributions and to be loud about it. I found that if I didn't speak up to discuss what I had done, or even the things that I aspired to do, as a Black woman, I would be left in a supportive role. I would be left watching someone else execute the ideas that I cultivated, simply because they knew that they could claim space that I was too timid to take for myself.

I also learned to ask for what I think I am worth instead of what others think I'm worth. As Black people, undervaluing ourselves is something that we have inherited from previous generations. Our ancestors had no choice but to labour in oppressive conditions that offered no reward. And even today, Black people continue to be underpaid, undervalued and economically disadvantaged. This holds true in acute ways in the nonprofit sector. If I want to be compensated in a way that is equitable, I must first ensure that I know what this means and be bold enough to demand it.

At various points along my journey to finding my voice, I was crippled by the fear of the unknown. But fear is the enemy of freedom. One has to be brave to break the chains of fear and grasp freedom for themselves. It is not something that anyone else can do for you. To obtain freedom you must act decisively and courageously, and then use your voice to empower, motivate and safeguard the path that will make freedom more attainable for the next generation. We simply cannot rest. There is much work to be done.

►●◄

Niambi Martin-John currently teaches in the nonprofit Leadership Management Post-Graduate Diploma Program at Seneca College and provides mentorship and coaching services to nonprofit boards, volunteers, and staff.

CHAPTER 9

Freedom in Discovery

HEBA MAHMOUD

"When I discover who I am, I'll be free."

—*Ralph Ellison*[30]

Ralph Ellison's *The Invisible Man* is a story about a nameless narrator who describes growing up in a Black community in the South, attending an all-Black college from which he is expelled, moving to New York and becoming the chief spokesman of the Harlem branch of a fictitious Black nationalist organization, before retreating to the basement lair of the Invisible Man, where he imagines himself to be amid race riots. The book was required reading in my ninth grade AP English class, one of my favorite subjects, not just because I loved to read and write, but because I loved the discussion we had about the themes that extended beyond our small high school classroom. An optimistic dreamer, I often wondered what our world could and should be, as I read pages and pages about what our world once was.

The Invisible Man was the basis of our class discussion on a spring day in 1998. As we passionately discussed identity in relation to societal and cultural norms, I remember turning to my best friend, a 15-year-old bi-racial American girl, and saying, "Wow, as Black women, it seems we are on the bottom rung of the power hierarchy!" She tipped her head to the side and gave me a pensive smirk. I wasn't prepared for what came next.

"YOU'RE at the bottom," she said pointing at me, *"at least I was born in America."*

I flinched as if I had been slapped. As she turned back to the class discussion, I remember my throat tightening with a lump, tears filling my eyes, and shame heating my cheeks with embarrassment. I felt anger zipping down my arms and legs as I started shaking. How could my best friend, the closest person to me, think I'm beneath her because I wasn't born in the United States? That was the first time I became hyper-aware of my identity.

As the days passed, I was stuck in that moment. I reflected on my life experiences; my family, my friends, where I lived. Who was I? I was born in Athens, Greece to Nubian Egyptian parents. Nubians are an ethnic group in Egypt, with our own language and customs that historians trace back to the Ancient Egyptians. My mother and I moved back to Egypt when I was two, where we lived with my grandmother and uncles for three years. My mother and I then moved to Washington, DC when I was five years old to live with my father. I have two siblings, both born in the US and both much younger than me.

I was never ashamed of being an immigrant. I was well respected in my close-knit Nubian Egyptian community, and as I became fluent in English, I was the official translator for many of my parents' friends. Outside of the Nubian community, I made friends with most everyone because I always had at least one thing in common with each student in my culturally diverse schools. So, why now, at the age of 15, was I questioning who I was in response to my best friend's comment?

After that incident in English class, I sat with those feelings of shame, anger, and confusion. I dissected and analyzed how each of my individual characteristics intersected to make me the person I am. After that reflection, I decided that I would not be ashamed to be an immigrant. I would not allow one conversation to tarnish my pride in my unique culture. I decided that I would become a vocal immigrant. I wrote stories and poems of my life experiences, which were published in our school's creative writing magazine. I signed up for every cultural appreciation event in high school. I belly-danced in our cultural showcase every year, but not alone, I taught my non-Egyptian friends the dances and we performed together.

A graduation requirement was to conduct a year-long research project and present the findings to a panel at the end of the school year. I researched Nubian-Egyptian wedding rituals for a full year. On the day of the presentation, I decorated the stage with Nubian prints. My biracial best friend and others dressed in traditional Nubian clothing and posed as a wedding party. I burned Nubian incense, played Nubian music, and offered Nubian food as I presented my research to a panel of my teachers. I received an Outstanding, the highest grade possible, and my project was featured on our school's website.

> Intersectionality was coined in 1989 by professor Kimberlé Crenshaw to describe how race, class, gender, and other individual characteristics "intersect" with one another and overlap.

While high school was my first tangible experience embracing my intersectional diversity, it wasn't the last. After graduating from high school, I attended Howard University, a historically Black university located in Washington, DC. There, I met people from all over the US and other countries around the world. My world opened up even more.

For the first time, people asked me *"Where are you from?"*

How did I answer that? "I am Nubian-Egyptian-American. Born in Greece and raised in the US" seemed too long. To keep it simple, I answered with "Arlington, VA," but was met with, *"No, where are you really from? You look ethnic."*

My first semester was consumed with figuring out how to answer that question. I finally perfected my answer in a way that felt most comfortable to me, "I am Nubian Egyptian and was raised in Arlington, VA." That response opened the door to an even deeper exploration of my intersectional background.

The African American students responded with, *"Oh, so you're African. How come you don't hang out with the*

African students?"

The African students responded with, *"Oh, so you're Arab. You're not really African."*

Here again, I was being *told* where my place was in the world. I was being shown that although I fit into each of those categories I didn't really fit with either group fully. This time around, however, I didn't feel anger and shame. I recognized the challenge that I had to overcome. Much like my high school experience, I set out to do the same in college. I became friends with everyone. I no longer was just the African or the Arab, but I was Heba. My time at Howard University was one of the most fun, eye-opening, and educational experiences of my life.

After completing my undergraduate degree, I started a career in Association and Nonprofit Management. As I began graduate school, and became a volunteer in my local community, I was again met with the same questions about my identity and life-experience, and each time, I overcame the forces that wanted to put me in a box. I became friends with people from various backgrounds and experiences while developing deeper empathy to better understand a variety of people. Where I once translated one language to another for family members, I now found myself translating my intersectional life experiences for others to better understand me.

In 2007, at the insistence of my family and in keeping with our cultural tradition, I faced my next life challenge. Through an arrangement, I met a Nubian Egyptian man from my tribe, who had a good family, and a good job. We married and I moved to Egypt, but using my voice to overcome challenges became increasingly difficult. For the next nine years, more intersections were added to my identity, including wife, daughter-in-law, mother, teacher, life coach, hijabi, ex-hijabi, divorcee, single parent, head of household, and domestic abuse survivor.

I lost my voice and my passion for everything. I stopped writing. I lost my sense of self and pride in my identity. More than that — overwhelmed with anger, grief, and shame and stemming from my failed marriage, I didn't know who I was anymore.

In 2010, I moved back to the US, this time with my son, and started working at an association advancing the fundraising profession. I was quickly promoted within the organization and my role was expanded giving me greater responsibility and the opportunity to work with volunteer leaders.

Newly divorced in 2016, I began working on the association's diversity and inclusion portfolio and met Birgit Smith Burton, an African American woman who'd been working as a fundraiser for more than twenty years. She was just stepping into her new role as volunteer chair of the association's diversity and inclusion committee. We began collaborating.

Birgit's calm and playful demeanor pushed me out of my shell. She encouraged me to share my ideas. She was a vocal supporter and advocate for me. Birgit accepted me for who I am, beyond my traumatic experiences. She led with compassion and vision. She inspired me. Through her presence she gave me space and permission to once again find my voice and use it.

Under Birgit's leadership and working with other

passionate volunteers, we advanced the association's diversity and inclusion initiatives. We launched an initiative to address the inequity issues facing women working as fundraisers in the nonprofit sector. We made equity a strategic focus for the association, which began to address the needs of women, in particular women of colour. Now four years later, Birgit will make history as the first female African American chair-elect of the Board of Directors of that same fundraising association.

Since meeting Birgit, I've been privileged to continue my career as a diversity and inclusion professional with other associations and nonprofit organizations. I help charitable organizations ensure they are diverse, inclusive, equitable, and accessible so they can reflect the communities they serve.

Charitable organizations play an important role in society and as such they should reflect their community. I believe we all have a role to play in giving back and making the world a better place. Important in this process is a more accurate picture of the philanthropic sector. One that reveals Black philanthropists and Black fundraisers. One that does not cast Black and brown people as only beneficiaries of charity. Diversity, equity, and inclusion work ensures the stories of Black people are shared and used to inform the systems we live and work in. New generations of leaders entering the workforce should see themselves reflected across the entire philanthropic spectrum.

At the end of *The Invisible Man*, the unnamed character shares that after years of hiding, he is ready to return to the world because he has spent enough time hiding from it. Hoping people will see past his invisibility, he shares his story to give voice to people with a similar plight.

My passion in the areas of diversity and inclusion helped me remember that my voice still has value, even after years of suppressing it. Using my voice helps create space for others, for people who are excluded, so they can step away from the margins of society and share their own stories. Like the Invisible Man, I know my purpose is to continue discovering who I am and the freedom that comes with it.

> *"Who knows but that, on the lower frequencies, I speak for you?"*
>
> —*Ralph Ellison*[31]

►●◄

Heba Mahmoud is the senior manager of diversity initiatives at the Consumer Technology Association. She holds a Bachelor of International Business and Marketing from Howard University and a Master of Business Management from Strayer University.

CHAPTER 10

In 'Us' I Find Freedom

CAMILA VITAL NUNES PEREIRA

Talking about my experience as a fundraiser is not easy for me.

I have been involved in the nonprofit sector for about five years and, in some ways, I am still trying to find my footing. I am definitely committed to the work, but struggle at times with the lack of opportunities for people that look like me — Black people — the lack of professional development, recognition and advancement, and many other disadvantages.

But I know these issues are not new.

When I reflect about my experiences, I always think about where I come from, my background, who I am and why all of these matters. These shape my understanding of the world, my purpose as an individual, my role in our communities, and ultimately the impact I would like to make and the legacy I want to leave.

From an early age I had to face and understand
the inequities in society — in this case Brazilian society — especially regarding Black people and their inability
to be their true selves and to be free. That fight for equity
continues in Brazil, but also in Canada, where I now live
and work. For me, this has emphasized the power of
systemic racism and inequality on a global scale.

Growing up in Brazil, I understood from a very young
age that I was part of a system in a society that had very
strict definitions of class, race and gender, and how each
relate. As a Black family, it was expected we would fit
into a predetermined category in society, including the
roles we were supposed to play and the expectation of
our lives. We would be part of the lower class, attend
public school, most likely not go to university (but, if
so, we were expected to attend a private one[32]), and
live in the outskirts of the city (where usually the cost
of living is lower). All of this is based on the dreadful
social, cultural and economic heritage of over 300 years
of slavery[33], with only a handful of social policies in
place to date for the advancement of Black people. My
parents knew if they wanted to empower us, education
would be the key to our freedom.

First, they would have to break the social paradigms,
challenge stereotypes, and make choices that would lead
them to challenge the status quo. While many of my
relatives would invest in their first homes from an early
age, my parents were not able to buy their own home
until the age of 45 because they chose to invest in many
years of education for their children. They began by
giving us a better education in a private school[34], and

then made sure we lived in a central location with easier access to the school and resources.

Next, they sat down with me and my siblings — I have a younger brother and an older sister (we are very close in age), to have important conversations about race and racism almost on a daily basis. They believed these were fundamental conversations so we could have an understanding of our roots, our history, our struggles and be prepared for the many challenges that we would face by being in spaces not meant for us. At the same time these talks instilled in us the power to truly believe we could be our true selves, free to be and do what we set our minds to. This was also part of their own journey as individuals, as parents and as partners. Many times, we would see and feel how uncomfortable those around us were, and how they were not always willing to have a relationship with us.

I was the only Black person in a classroom for most of my school years (Another Black girl finally showed up in my last year of high school.). Being the only one forces you to create many mechanisms, some initially to simply survive; then others to challenge and have your voice heard; and finally others that help you ignore the many things that are done to hurt you, oppress you and disregard your presence. Yet other mechanisms helped me rise above, excel and develop the courage to push back and break the constricting paradigms and stereotypes in order to create space for me and other Black people to be fully ourselves.

So why is this so important as I reflect and share my experiences with you?

When I arrived in Canada after living in the United States for about nine years, where I attended graduate school at Howard University — a historically Black university and a remarkable experience in itself — I had a vision of Canada being a very diverse country and welcoming to immigrants, which on the surface it certainly seemed to be.

However, after looking for a job for a few months without success I learned about the necessary requirement of "Canadian experience." I debated this "chicken-or-egg" cycle with a friend, because if you can't get an opportunity, you can't get any Canadian experience, which of course frustrated me, as it seemed to be a perfect Catch-22. I also received feedback a few times that I was too educated, and I should exclude my doctoral degree from my résumé. I was advised to focus on more junior positions to get my foot in the door somewhere, and then build up my career.

Well, omitting my degree was definitely not an option. In fact, I considered that suggestion offensive, and wondered if that was a recommendation made regularly to white immigrants (unlikely!). Why, I thought, would someone try to fit me back in the Black Brazilian stereotype I had worked so hard to break away from? Some might say I was just a "lucky girl," but I wanted to show that I could do whatever I set my mind to, to show my excellence and power, and to influence other girls like me to dream big.

"Lucky implies that I was handed something I did not earn, that I did not work hard for I am not lucky. You

know what I am? I am smart, I am talented, I take
advantage of the opportunities that come my way and
I work really, really hard. Don't call me lucky. Call
me a badass."

— *Shonda Rhimes* [35]

One thing was becoming clear. Regardless of any of my achievements, my gender and my colour were definitely speaking louder, and much of what I had accomplished was just being diminished, disregarded or discarded. This was creating a lot of conflict within me.

When I first entered the nonprofit sector, I remember being excited because of my passion to have meaningful impact and spark change, especially in diverse and Black communities. I immediately noticed that the organization I worked for was not very diverse. Initially it didn't upset me; it was a familiar environment. But I had been expecting a *different* experience, especially in the diverse, multicultural city of Toronto. I had assumed Torontonians had embraced diversity…but I certainly wasn't seeing that in my organization or in the sector.

I found myself often facing micro-aggressions from colleagues. They made references to my education, suggesting that I had wasted my time in school. They made comments about my English proficiency and would sometimes approach me to make sure I had understood certain parts of a conversation. They even referred to my Brazilian background with derogatory and racist comments referring to Black women and their objectification in Brazil. It was overwhelming and exhausting, and I needed many deep breaths to stem the roller coaster of emotions in those moments.

Often I would respond to these aggressions, as my mom would say, with 'grace', and try to 'educate' them about my racial and cultural background in Brazil. Other times I just got irritated. I disliked being obliged to prove myself, explain myself, fight for a 'seat' at the table and have my voice heard. It was painful, and it didn't seem to matter how good I was at doing my job. Any recognition I received would be followed by comments about my identity, my background and the need for me to 'fit' more within the Canadian cultural norms. It was definitely a *ginormous* challenge…how could I 'fit' into a culture that does not represent me? I wondered where the history of Black people within the Canadian culture was told. And what about the history of Black fundraisers and nonprofit professionals? I didn't understand.

Now of course, you are likely shaking your head and saying, *"girl you don't have to 'fit' in,"* and of course you are absolutely right, I do not have to fit in; these spaces were not made for me.

Often, it has been too difficult to address some issues. Those instances would immediately bring me back to my childhood, when my mom would emphasize the importance of standing up for ourselves, not letting our race or gender speak higher than our truth and our beliefs. But, how do you to do that when you have so much at stake? I had friends who lost their jobs because they were vocal about racism and the dissatisfaction they felt in their jobs. How do you stand up when you are feeling alone? Should you take that risk?

I have always had the courage to voice and stand up for what I believe, but at a younger age it was easier when I had a strong support system to lift me up. This was different, however, and circumstances can change everything. Some circumstances challenge you personally, and after a while for me, doubt crept in. I found myself overthinking past career decisions. This was uncomfortable, and forced me to rethink my career choice in the nonprofit sector. A very good friend of mine said,

> *Camila, you bring such unique experience and insights to our work; don't let them affect your passion and commitment, because the work you do is from your heart and done with excellence. Some spaces are just not ready for people like us (she is also Black) and they will try to suppress and oppress us by undermining our work and our contribution; we can decide to leave those organizations and go elsewhere where they see us and value us more.*

> *"As Black women, we're always given these seemingly devastating...experiences that could absolutely break us. But what the caterpillar calls the end of the world, the master calls the butterfly. What we do as Black women is take the worst situations and create from that point."*

> —*Viola Davis*

One thing I knew for sure was that I had to bring my full self back; I wanted to, and I needed to find my freedom, but part of me was missing. I was doing work that I believed in, but something was missing. I wanted to belong. To feel part of a community, a community that would have my back and understand where I am coming from, a community that could understand my struggles and challenges. I was missing a place where I could be my true self.

Even though I had often been the only one in a room from an early age, I had always had a strong support system in my family. So where is the Black Brazilian community support today? I was never involved with the Black community growing up, but my family was greatly involved in charitable initiatives benefiting Black children. My lack of involvement with the Black Brazilian community was not a matter of choice; it was rather due to a lack of opportunity. My family lived in an environment where Black people were small in number and we were just trying to make it and succeed in life.

To fuel my soul and continue my journey in the nonprofit sector I was eager to meet and expand my network…to meet more fundraisers like me, but how to do that? Then I came across a fellowship program with the Association of Fundraising Professionals. I applied and got accepted, and it was a turning point for me where I found my freedom again.

"Freedom is acquired by conquest, not by gift. It must be pursued constantly and responsibly. Freedom is not an ideal located outside of man; nor is it an idea which becomes myth. It is rather the indispensable condition for the quest for human completion."

— *Paulo Freire* [36]

Over a period of a few months, I met fantastic fund-raisers through workshops I attended and courses we took together—as Fellows in the program, and through projects on which we collaborated. Through my fellowship mentor Nneka Allen, I joined the Black Canadian Fundraisers Collective. What a joy! Every gathering was so fulfilling, and our gatherings were a delight. It was a joy to be together with Black women, sharing their experiences of pain and stories of love. We supported each other; it was most needed.

This inspiring community brought me back to myself and awakened my beliefs. I started feeling whole again. The voices of Black women are strong and required; we are not the problem. We are beyond excellent. We are powerful. We bring unique experience and contributions to our work. This community—my community—brought me back to freedom, to be my full self, to engage with all my heart in this sector and to speak my truth always.

Today and tomorrow, it is our time to share our stories and who we are as nonprofit professionals. It is time to claim our seat at the table or build our own table—many places are not yet ready for us, but we are not waiting any longer. It is our time to make change happen together. It is our time to embrace our vulnerabilities, to lift each other, and to learn with one another. It is time for us to embrace our freedom and let it speak truth to power.

"Truth is powerful and it prevails."

—*Sojourner Truth*

Let us all embrace our freedom and accomplish our dreams. We are active players in this process, in this movement — our movement — and together we are building our legacy, writing our history, challenging the status quo, and dismantling structures such as institutional racism that were built to keep us on the sidelines. We are breaking standards and paving new ways for those coming into the nonprofit and philanthropic sector.

> *"For to be free is not merely to cast off one's chains, but to live in a way that respects and enhances the freedom of others."*

> —*Nelson Mandela*

►●◄

Camila Vital Nunes Pereira is a fundraising professional in Toronto and a coach to Brazilians involved in philanthropy and fundraising in Brazil and Canada. She holds a PhD in Public Policy/Public Administration & International Relations from Howard University.

LOVE

CHAPTER 11

My Love for Philanthropy

FATOU JAMMEH

"Money is like love; it kills slowly and painfully the one who withholds it, and enlivens the other who turns it on his fellow man."

—*Kahlil Gibran*

I can still remember the first time I held a cheque for one million dollars in my hand.

As a young fundraiser making less than five percent of this cheque a year, I couldn't begin to imagine what this amount of wealth meant. Yet here I was, holding a piece of paper as light as a feather with enormous power to change lives, even the lives of those of us in the headquarters. Thinking back now about how this gift was secured through a simple coffee conversation is alluring for me. I too wanted to talk to wealth, see what this sector of philanthropy was about and how it could effect change.

Pursuing philanthropy has been an interesting journey. For a long time, my heart longed to advocate for resources for those in need. In the beginning I wasn't sure what area I would do this work in, but my first two jobs as a fundraiser were with women's rights organizations. At the time, I thought this was it; my desires have been met.

Little did I know that my journey had just begun. Since then I've had various roles and have come to realize that it's not simply about the cause or the particular organization. It is also about my motivation, my love for humanity, my wish for equity and my quest for a level playing field.

The Greek etymological meaning of the word "philanthropy" involves love (*phil*) of humanity (*anthropos*). Love in the philanthropic sector for a Black fundraiser like myself is a feeling that is hard to find. Outwardly, we do excellent work, and in some instances we "save lives." Today, five years into the profession, when I ask myself if I feel the love I can say yes. But it hasn't always been that way. It took me four years of tackling barriers and challenges to get to this point.

Early in my career, I saw firsthand how nonprofits treated their employees, especially Black and brown people. This treatment did not align with their stated values. Institutional racism was an overt fact against which little action was taken. When I spoke to an executive leader about the revolving door of people in their organization and the lack of diversity among their leaders, the answer was that the qualified prospective leaders could not be found in persons from diverse backgrounds. What a remarkable and revelatory response!

How could I really love this sector when I had to fight to have love reciprocated? It was difficult for me to view philanthropy as love for humanity when predominately white people, who hold the power to give this love through monetary resources, are the same people using it to exclude and disadvantage people like me.

When I spoke up about the marginalization of Black and brown bodies in the charitable sector, the organization's response was to censor my voice, even as they perpetuated an external image of bestowing love. I was really shocked and stunned at the hypocrisy. It was a traumatic lesson. The organization was supposed to be committed to fighting for the rights of people who lack a platform from which to speak out. Ironically, there I was speaking up and being shut down.

Talking about love in a space where love is absent is hard, but I came to understand the structure of philanthropy, its resources, and the allocation of wealth. And what I have discovered is how the wealthy are comfortable making pledges to fundraisers who look like them. And they are uncomfortable making pledges to fundraisers like me, a Black African woman who does not look like them.

At one point, I really didn't know if I would continue on a path in the philanthropic sector. As a Black African fundraiser, I have not encountered the wealth of individuals like Gates, Rockefellers or Carnegies. In fact, I didn't even know who they were until my work in philanthropy began. Growing up, my trajectory was to obtain a position in a traditional role such as a teacher, doctor or lawyer, with the goal of enhancing my life and my family's. I am the first fundraiser in my family and saw this as an opportunity to extend love further into my community. I also know this is true for many other Black people in the sector.

I, like other Black fundraisers, experience ostracization as I navigate racially-fraught power dynamics and endure affronts to my dignity. But I still have a firm belief that Black fundraisers are well aligned and suited to command space in this sector. It is critical that we use our collective voices to advocate for the interests of people who sit on the margins within our communities. In doing so, we can find healing and love in our collective strength. Together, we occupy a position of influence. Not only do we raise money, but also we can guide where it goes and what gets funded.

One thing I know about the power of love is that it has the ability to heal us. And I find healing through my ability to meet the needs of others. I am grateful when I am able to share love by holding healing space for other fundraisers of colour. It's important to me that I can be an advocate and a support. Another contribution I am currently supporting is the auditing of policies in my organization for gaps in relation to equity, fairness and racial diversity…issues that will affect the inclusion of Black fundraisers.

As I journey forward, I am aware of the barriers that still exist for Black fundraisers. The key to a systemic shift critical in achieving the change we desire is to understand our power and our value in the nonprofit sector. I'm now convinced that for any real change to happen, we must contribute to the dismantling of systems and institutions, and I'm doing my part by starting within my own realm of influence. As Edgar Villaneuva concludes in *Decolonizing Wealth*, "philanthropy as the sector most ostensibly responsible for healing, could and should lead the way".[37]

I will continue on this journey of healing and love through philanthropy. I will continue to create spaces where we all feel that we belong, where our opinions matter, where philanthropy is used as a tool for liberation and where we have equal access. Here's to the love of the work of philanthropy for the sake of humanity and to welcoming love with open arms.

"When we engage in acts of love, we humans are at our best and most resilient"

—adrienne maree brown[38]

▶●◀

Fatou Jammeh has worked in various fundraising capacities for several organizations including Doctors Without Borders (MSF), UNICEF Canada, The Match Fund and the Women's Legal Aid Centre. With a Bilingual Degree in International Studies from York University and a Certificate in Inclusion and Philanthropy from AFP Canada, Fatou has lived and worked in Canada, Tanzania, France and Gambia, and speaks English, French, and Mandinka.

CHAPTER 12

Love Lifted Me

BIRGIT SMITH BURTON

Ursula's Unconditional Love

I don't remember her face. The woman through whom God gave me life.

Her name was Ursula Schmidt.

For years I searched for her face in my mind, my heart, and in my dreams. I could *feel* her in the depths of my being.

I remember how she smelled, like honeysuckle. I used to smell it in my sleep and wake up looking for her. A whiff of someone's perfume on the street would spin me around hoping to find her.

As a little child, I spoke German, it was my first language.

I would call for my mother sometimes, "Mutti! Mutti!!"

I knew she loved me. I had no doubt. I remember feeling the love. Deep love. I don't remember what she said to me the day before she gave me away on that late summer day in Germany—August 8th to be exact—to my new mom and dad. I was two and a half.

Later I would understand that she desperately wanted me to be with a family where I would not have a miserable life because of the color of my skin. She had kept me with her after I was born on May 3rd until the day my new parents picked me up from the Kinderheim, the children's home.

How much love did she have for me, to make the heart-wrenching decision to give me away for *selfless* reasons? I looked at my son when he turned two and a half and imagined giving him away. For a million *selfish* reasons, I could not.

A Family Built Through Love

How much love does it take to love someone else's child? Charles and Angie Smith, my adoptive parents, gave me a ton of it. Enough love to last a lifetime after they passed away, making up for the loss of my birth mother and the sadness of recently finding my birth father and enduring his denial when he announced to me, *"I have only three daughters,"* and rattled off their names, *"...and not four."*

On the *SS United States*, the ship that we sailed on across the Atlantic Ocean to my new home in America, I was hugged and kissed and cuddled and adorned in pretty dresses and perfect bows by my new parents. They made me feel special. They were so happy to have a child of their own after ten years of marriage. My dad was an officer in the Air Force and he and my mother decided, while stationed in Germany, to adopt a child. Oddly, I recall the first few days with them. The happiness and joy. Riding stretched out in their small sports car with my head in my mother's lap and feet in my dad's. I clutched a new stuffed panda tightly in my arms sent to me by my cousin Tommy who was also adopted and waiting anxiously to meet me back in the United States. Somehow, I knew this love was just an extension of the love from my birth mother. Yet I had no idea what love was about to come into my life.

A Grandmother's Love

My grandmother taught me early on what it meant to love and care for people—to give of yourself. I know that her love of people existed long before I met her, but for me, it began the day that my parents brought me from Germany to a small Southwest Michigan town called Covert. And if you've heard of Covert, then we're probably related. I remember a big white house and my grandmother greeting us—me, mom and dad—at the back door with more love, hugs and squeezes than one little three-year-old could handle. She seemed so happy to see me and I accepted it, although I didn't quite understand it. We went inside the house into her kitchen and there began a twenty-year relationship with the most amazing woman I have ever known. They called her Reverend Alvene Grice. Some called her pastor. Some called her sis or mother. Mutt was another name although I have no idea where that name came from. My cousins and I called her Poppy. (It's a long story).

So, Poppy pastored a church in the small town of Covert, and whenever I visited I would excitedly hop into her car and get as close to her as possible while we drove all around the community making stops to visit with people. I didn't know what we were doing, I just knew people were so happy to see her. Years later I learned she brought food and clothing. Often she would pray, and sometimes she would just hug them.

She was also known for going to the school and visiting classrooms to brush and comb the hair of children whose parents had not done so before sending them to school. While she had the children's attention, she would tell them how important it is to get a college education. And on Sunday mornings Poppy would transform into a majestic woman in the pulpit to deliver a sermon with all of the fervor and passion she could bring forth to a whopping crowd of maybe 150 people — at capacity — with standing room only. I felt so proud to be her granddaughter and I wanted to be just like her.

My grandmother passed away when I was 24. The town of Covert is so small that the last of the cars were still exiting the church parking lot from her funeral as the hearse was entering the cemetery. My heart was broken, but I knew that in some way I would carry out my grandmother's work. Thousands of miles from where love began for me, I realized that love would take me down a path towards a career that would make absolute sense. Being a champion for those that needed my help.

Birgit, Loving Myself

While interning at a minority-owned advertising agency, (I was completing my degree in media communications) I had the opportunity to help plan a celebrity golf tournament for the United Negro College Fund (UNCF). I didn't know much about UNCF at the time except the slogan *"A Mind is a Terrible Thing to Waste,"* which had made me laugh and ask, is a mind really a *terrible* thing?

What was most fascinating to me was the existence of an organization solely for the education of Black people. I was drawn to the mission and excited that this golf tournament would raise money to ensure more Black students would obtain a college degree. It took me back to my grandmother's message to the students while combing their hair—go to college. I was intrigued and encouraged to explore what fundraising was all about and how this might be the career for me, especially if I could do this *and* benefit people of color.

As it turned out, UNCF was looking for me!

Young Black college graduates with an interest in learning about the fundraising field. What amazing luck!

They took a chance on me, and I spent the next eleven years honing my skills as a regional development officer and raising millions of dollars for Black colleges and universities. But it wasn't as easy as I thought it would be. I experienced so much racism and negativity. Especially in the north where there weren't any UNCF-supported schools. One white woman called my office to complain after she had seen an advertisement on television for our upcoming telethon.

"Why do Black people need separate schools? That's the entire issue. If they attended better schools, they would have a better education and they wouldn't have so many problems."

I asked her where she had attended college.

"I didn't go to college," she confessed.

After UNCF, I accepted a job at the Georgia Institute

of Technology. I was certain this would be an easier gig, since this was a prestigious university. Raising money from private foundations for "minority" students and programs at Georgia Tech would be a breeze.

Not so fast.

It had not occurred to me that the potential barrier to my success would not be the color of the skin of the people for whom I would raise money, but rather the color of my own skin! I had *no* idea that I would be the first Black front-line fundraiser hired at Georgia Tech. And one afternoon I had the misfortune of sitting next to an alum at a scholars' luncheon—he was about 85 years old—and he proudly proclaimed how he recalled the "good-ole-days" when there were no Blacks or women at Georgia Tech.

One evening I looked hard at my face in the mirror. I looked at the color of my skin. Brown. The issue of my brown skin had followed me from birth. At every turn. There were times at school I had been bullied because I was brown. I had been passed over for theatrical roles because I was brown. I had my heart shattered by my first love because I was brown. Yet, underneath the pain that my brown skin had brought me was the underlying love that has lifted me and given me the strength and courage to be bold and proud of whom I am. The strength to love *me*. That strength and love gave me the audacity to know I could have a career and be successful in my brown skin.

Love of Mankind

I'm often invited to bring a keynote speech at conferences or major events, or to serve on panels or interview about my journey in the fundraising profession. And the story of my life I usually tell is not the one about my mother. I tell the other story of my life, switching from a planned Broadway career — I studied voice and held roles in high school productions and community dinner theater — to broadcast journalism and ultimately fundraising

Fundraiser?

How does one go from performing arts to begging for money? Well, it was quite a journey that ended up with me stumbling into a career I knew nothing about and landing in an organization that was willing to hire me and teach me how to fundraise. And I discovered that I love raising money for people and organizations whose needs are met by my efforts. And I don't just *love raising* money but going a bit deeper, I love people.

And what is the definition of philanthropy?

"The love of humankind."

So, before I stumbled into the fundraising profession, I did have an inkling that I cared for people, and looking back I know exactly where that came from, without hesitation. I know it was love that brought me to my passion.

∞

Loving the Difference I Can Make

I acknowledge my journey in fundraising and how love has molded, inspired, and guided me. I have spent my adult life volunteering for organizations that support people of color and mirror my grandmother's passion — especially my service with Hosea Feed the Hungry and Homeless. And to support my fundraising brothers and sisters of color in the profession, I created the African American

Development Officers (AADO) Network. Now nearly 2,500 members strong, AADO celebrates the hard work of those Black and brown professionals who deserve to be recognized and supported for what they accomplish every day, against all odds, to make a difference in the world.

I am blessed and grateful for the way that love has been the guiding force in my life, leading me on a journey of twists and turns because of the color of my skin, but ultimately allowing me to make a difference despite it.

To honor my grandmother and carry out her legacy, I helped establish the Alvene E. Lowe Grice Memorial Scholarship Fund which to date has provided scholarships for hundreds of students from Covert High School to attend college.

"Love recognizes no barriers. It jumps hurdles, leaps fences, penetrates walls to arrive at its destination full of hope."

—*Maya Angelou*

►●◄

Birgit Smith Burton is the executive director for Foundation Relations at Georgia Tech, co-authored The Philanthropic Covenant with Black America, and is current chair-elect for the Association of Fundraising Professionals' global board. She earned her BA in media communications from Medaille College in Buffalo, New York.

CHAPTER 13

Stretto

NAIMAH BILAL

The fugue has meaning to me on a personal level because classical music was my first on-ramp into a world of whiteness.

A fugue is a contrapuntal composition in which a short melody or phrase (the subject) is introduced by one part and successively taken up by others and developed by interweaving the parts. The word fugue is derived from the Latin work *fuga* meaning "to flee."

My formative years were marked by on-ramps and off-ramps between two very different worlds: one world, my community, marked by a scarcity of wealth, and another, Georgetown, where my music school was located, marked by opulent wealth. Three days a week my mother would ferry me to and from our modest apartment in Southeast to the gilded Colonials and Federal-style homes so characteristic of this posh Washington DC neighborhood.

Violin lessons, chamber music, orchestra, and music theory offered me windows into a world of creativity and art that I craved as a child. The halls in which I studied and concertized offered few mirrors that could reflect back to me who I was, but one of my most enduring gifts from that experience has been the ability to connect with people through the power of music.

On a practical level, the fugue is an effective metaphor to reveal the complexities and transmutations of experience amid changing conditions, orientations, and settings. And there is no irony lost to reference a white compositional tradition to tell my Black story.

For me, a touchstone of deep human connection is the enlightened awareness that can emerge when seemingly disparate elements commingle, and a deeply-shared understanding and unity can come about. The unique challenge for me has been trying to convey the meaning of my encounters of inequity as a Black woman working in the field of philanthropy. The challenge persists not for lack of words to express the experience; rather the friction is the dissonance arising when juxtaposing those harmful experiences alongside the ethos of modern Western philanthropy as an agent of social good.

In many ways, when set next to those you will read in this anthology, my own narrative may feel like a variation on a theme. You, the reader, will recognize patterns of inequity and pick out rhythms of discrimination without redress. I hope that my story can both illuminate the journey of one Black philanthropoid and offer a coda of hope, healing, and transformation for the future of our field.

The Fugue Subject — My Philanthropic North Star

As I process my earliest orienting to the world of philanthropy, my memory is of attending church as a child.

Alms-giving was preached as a vital function of community well-being, and the manifestations of these voluntary gifts were visible on all levels. Tithing from one service alone would yield a scholarship for a rising freshman off to university. A collection on another Sunday might provide meals for the "sick and shut-in" and the congregation's seniors. Alms-giving for community elevation, care, and advancement was the immutable North Star guiding my conception of how unbridled love for humankind is demonstrated. And donations were placed in unmarked envelopes, as giving was taught to be an act of anonymity, summoning next-level magnanimity.

In our fugue, we can think of this North Star as the 'tonal center'—which in music is the 'Optimus Prime' of pitches, amid a hierarchy of pitches organized within a particular key. The tonal center orients the listener to these pitches, and a strong presence of this center signals a magnetic pull toward stability and idealized alignment.

Imitation in the Fugue — Interrogating Ethos

As my experience with social good work expanded outside of this idealized church-going bubble, I entered into a new register of awareness as to the duality of philanthropy.

My first professional foray into fundraising was (surprise!) with a performing arts organization—an orchestra of tremendous repute. There, I was trained to raise transformative gifts to secure the long-term sustainability of the institution. The appeal to give generously in support of a public good was recognizable to me. And it was within this framing I found an abiding love for the work to help donors do with our institution what they could not do alone. At the edges of this early experience, though, was an emerging dissonance to which, over time, I could not abide.

First, I began to comprehend that donor motivation expanded well beyond a magnanimous call to give for the common good, and that these motivations had varying proximities to a core of virtue ethics. Some donors gave for the sake of the common good, others because they felt a need to belong, and others still because they wanted to be recognized for their contributions. All three fall pretty squarely along the Maslowian spectrum of needs, making them all fair game as virtuously-rooted motivations for giving.

A disquieting reaction set in for me when we were taught to activate yet other motivations for giving that had less to do with meeting a natural human need but rather centered on human desires for access, power, and privilege. In spite of this challenge to my ethical framing, I began to understand and would later master the skill of actuating those motivations — at the level of scale — to secure gifts.

Our drive for resource efficiency also energized a culture of patronage to power whereby the wealthiest donors were assigned out-sized resources and value in our fundraising ecosystem. And sadly, this setting and the obvious ways in which this imbalance manifested began to obscure my North Star.

The PowerPoint decks we used for gift solicitation oriented donors to the 'perks' of giving. Impact, much less equity of impact, was an afterthought. In this way, the subject of the fugue was now muted. The counterpoint of voices was so ferocious as to make me question whether it would ever resolve to my North Star.

To the wealthiest donors, this approach gave rise to a culture that afforded them the deference and respect one might give to the Pope, while those who had given smaller gifts regularly were often unnoticed and under-recognized. The most monied donors were given access to cultural and political capital that donors positioned on the lower end of the donor pyramid wouldn't dream of experiencing without a few extra zeros added to their gift amounts.

In this community, the wealth gap between white and Black residents was stark so it was no surprise that the imbalance would be mirrored within the symphony's donor ecosystem. This inequity was further entrenched by a blinkered lens of philanthropy where treasure was king. Time and talent? Not so much.

At the top of the food chain were white arts patrons, and at the bottom Black patrons. In one stark illustration, a local Black businesswoman and well-regarded member of the community sponsored a production. Though her gift was modest by comparison to the fortune 500 corporations who sponsored other concerts, she introduced scores of new patrons to the symphony who might never have come were it not for her invitation. Back office commentary focused on the modesty of her giving, less so on the larger meaning of her gift as an influential Black arts patron who had a passion for the art form and a deep connection with the Black community.

As I dug deeper into my work, I experienced the tug and pull toward and away from my North Star. And as I began to seek professional growth in the nonprofit ranks, I would soon find myself personally entangled in elements of inequity that would awaken me to the ceilings of growth placed on Black nonprofit and fundraising professionals.

Development of the Fugue: This Woman's Work

Introspection into the meaning of a Black woman's efforts to develop and grow within the nonprofit space brings many thoughts to bear. First I conjure the image of a twenty-something me, seeking a pathway to growth in my job at a nonprofit I loved. Little did I know that expressing a desire to grow would draw the ire of my white male supervisor.

In his words, I was *"not a good cultural fit"* for the institution, and he would go on to enumerate his reasons I was not cut out for advancement. His biggest criticism: an absence from work to care for my then 1-year-old who had a serious case of pneumonia. *"Your absence from work exceeds that of your colleagues,"* he said. Though dumbfounded by his cold detachment from the fact that my child's mortality hung in the balance, I went to HR to check his assertion. I would later find out that not only had I underutilized paid-time-off, but that my white colleagues were afforded the opportunity to "bank" vacation days for family emergencies such as the ones I just had. One colleague, also a new mother, was even given the option to take Friday afternoons off to be home with her child. The only salient difference between us: our skin color. Whether intentional or not, the circumstances and the glaring disparities along racial lines implied one message: Black women can't advance here.

To say nothing of his people management skills, his lack of compassion revealed an intersectionalized discrimination that sounded with a dissonance that was too much for me to bear. Two weeks later, and after seven years of exemplary performance, I tendered my resignation. I couldn't square this sequence of events with an organization that, at least rhetorically, trumpeted the power of art to bring about unity, interconnectedness, and compassion. The mirroring of racist power structures within a construct of virtue and righteousness was plainly incompatible. My efforts then fixated on revealing this dissonance—giving voice to it—as any good fugist does.

In a fugue, the tonal center by design is obscured by transmutations of key and tonality. The tension that emerges from this interplay tests the will of the listener with episodes of cacophony and discord, leaving them feeling disoriented and detached from the aligned center.

When I made my exit from this institution, I devoted myself to finding my way back to alignment with a North Star illuminated by compassion, unity, truth, and love.

Stretto: Drawn Together in Alignment

The entrance of the stretto in a fugue is always a signal letting listeners know the end is near. Not in the ominous sense of the phrase, however, but in a way of having arrived back into a place of alignment. As we've seen on our sojourn, this arrival is inevitably preceded by an interplay of sometimes discordant musical material, superimposed over one another in a manner that causes conflicting harmonies.

We know a stretto is underway when we hear a fast entry of multiple melodic lines and voices—each entering before the prior voice has completed. This overlapping of material has the undeniable effect of creating a loud chorus of sound awakening the listener to a coming arrival.

In the last several years, a growing criticism of impropriety and inequity in the philanthropic edifice has risen to a deafening roar. Much like our stretto, voices of journalists, academics, political activists, and philanthropists are converging to sound the alarm. As we witness a reckoning with the cumulative impacts of slavery, Jim Crow, and modern-day discrimination, we are also witnessing reckoning of immense proportions with the origin story of modern American philanthropy as the child of capitalism.

The unjust elements that exist within the fundraising edifice are so stark as to be shocking. The most scrutiny is trained on the insidious practice of reputation laundering—where just beneath the surface of a veneered magnanimity—is a nefarious desire of some would-be benefactors to distract us from the ill-gotten means through which their wealth was accumulated. Jeffrey Epstein and the Sackler Family come to mind.

Though it took media firestorms of epic proportions to erupt for change to happen, in both instances, institutions that accepted philanthropic gifts from these infamous funders have returned their gifts. The ugly truths that lie at the heart of our philanthropic work have at last been laid bare for us to behold. In an industry shot through with inequity that mirrors the worst aspects of our capitalist system, where can we find hope?

The optimism I bring to my work emanates from what I detect as a returning chorus aligned with truth and justice. As truth-telling aimed at interrogating the nature of power grows, we see more clearly power's natural propensity to perpetuate itself with still more power, all while covering itself with the cloak of philanthropy. However, recognition alone won't get us to a place of transformation and reform. We sit upon a structural problem that can only be addressed when we uproot the whole dang tree of racism, white supremacy, and their poisoned intersections with capitalism.

For now, my goal is to seek better alignment with my North Star in my own work by dismantling the levers of inequity within my reach to find harmonic resolution where I can. Residing deep within that North Star is my understanding that, in its highest form, philanthropy is a function of love. In the same way that a fugue is an expression of musical ideas, where the tonal center prevails at the end, I seek a philanthropic world that after a struggle of ideas, methods and values, lives up to its highest self.

►●◄

Naimah Bilal is a Washington, DC native, nonprofit leader, and fundraising executive. She received her BA and MA at Indiana University Bloomington and Case Western Reserve University. She is now pursuing her MBA with a concentration in Economics at the University of Cincinnati.

CHAPTER 14

Our Love is Our Only Freedom

NNEKA ALLEN

To my beloved Black Sisters and Brothers in the philanthropic sector,

Bigger than you, bigger than we
Bigger than the picture they framed us to see
Legacy

— *Beyonce, Black is King*

This is a letter of love from a daughter of the Underground Railroad.

It is with great respect that I write to you. I esteem what we have achieved by surviving in a world that dishonours and discredits Black voices.

As you read my words, may you remember our ancestral bonds that illuminate our boundless affection. May you remember the supernatural love that has been cultivated in our lives through our ancestors. The love that has survived atrocities and yet still abounds. Our familial bonds that have been decimated over history, and still love remains. This exceptional love legacy weaves precious threads through the tapestry of our lives. And many things can be achieved through our love, even freedom. History bears witness to this.

May my words also inspire you to always choose courage. I pray that you will have the courage to resist fear, courage to always raise your voice and courage to contribute your intelligence, your brilliance and your magic.

And while you, Brothers and Sisters, are my audience, in my words are also lessons for the "powerful" in the philanthropic sector. If the "leaders" of our sector tune into the spirit of my message they will discover many things about us, our love, our legacy and our largesse. If they listen and choose to receive the truth with humility, they will benefit from this story of caution. The gifts of Black people are abundant. And people with power would be wise to position themselves to receive from us the solutions we have conceived through pain and oppression and birthed in love.

Love does not begin and end the way we seem to think it does. Love is a battle; love is a war; love is a growing up.

— *James Baldwin, author and activist*

Love found me in 1999. Not passionate love. Not affectionate love. It was more profound. It was an enduring and omnipresent love. This love insisted that I stand firm. It wrapped me up in an affirmation that I belonged. It whispered, "You have greatness inside." It shouted, "You matter."

This is when I fell in love with my Blackness, my identity, my people and my history.

∞

After a decade of searching for my life's purpose, I fell into an opportunity to participate in a capital campaign to restore a monumental historic structure, the Nazrey African Methodist Episcopal (AME) Church, a sacred edifice that served many seeking spiritual comfort and consolation, and for nearly 20 years provided freedom from the oppression of slavery in the United States. Built in 1848 in Amherstburg, Ontario, it was an active part of the AME denomination, and like its sister churches throughout Canada and the United States, was also a station on the Underground Railroad (UGRR). Today, the Nazrey AME Church is designated a Canadian National Historic Site, and forms part of the Amherstburg Freedom Museum's properties (formerly the North American Black Historical Museum).

It was in this precise place that I discovered love for who I am.

The town of Amherstburg holds a unique place in the history of Canada. Although little-known, it sits at the narrowest part of the Detroit River across from Wyandotte, Michigan. It is noteworthy because many refugee slaves escaping slavery entered Canada in this small town because of the short distance to cross the river. Refugee slaves could cross the river either by swimming or walking across the ice in the winter. This is where my ancestors found freedom in the 1840s.

Like many fundraisers, I didn't begin my work at the Museum with a fundraiser's title, despite the distinct fundraising elements of my work. I was primarily hired to research and write a report for the federal government on the history and restoration of Nazrey. I now realize this report was stewardship for the major gift the federal government had contributed to the capital campaign.

While poring over primary documents for six months to understand the purpose, impact and history of Nazrey, I began understanding myself in new ways. Never in my life had I spent so much time reading and understanding the active role that Black families played in the robust and meticulous AME network. Nazrey was a safe house or way-station on the UGRR, and the names in the Nazrey archive were the names of station masters. All the names in the reports and documents were familiar and connected to me in some way. These men and women were devoted to the physical, mental and spiritual liberty of Black people.

"Although they had strange roads, woods and night scenes to pass through, yet they faltered not. They found friends and advisers on the road, however, and reached the Committee in safety…Heavy rewards were offered through advertisements in the Baltimore Sun, but they availed naught. The Vigilance Committee received them safely, fully cared for them, and safely sent them through to the land of refuge."

—William Still, abolitionist for the Vigilance Committee

A zealous love had come to life for me. I had never seen a Black activist organization up close and I was enraptured. After over two-and-a-half years at the Museum researching, writing, raising money and relearning history, I emerged with a heart fully affirmed in my Blackness. I will never forget that this love began for me in the heart of a nonprofit organization. This is where I became a fundraiser.

Sadly in 2001, I had to leave the Museum due to a decline in visitorship following the tragedy of 9/11. However, nine years later, in 2010, I was asked to return to the Museum as a board member, and I gladly accepted the invitation because this was the place where I had discovered my purpose…the place where my love for justice and equity had been cultivated. I saw this as a privilege and opportunity for me to pour the love I cultivated in my early career back into the organization that had first loved me. I had just achieved my Certified Fundraising Executive designation, and I was excited. Ready to work.

During the next five years, the Museum board nudged the organization in a more modern direction. But after some progress, it became evident to me that something more fundamental needed to change. As David Fleming pointed out,

> "The idea that museums can positively impact individuals' lives and bring benefit to society at large is one that has taken hold and gained increasing consensus across museum practitioners and policymakers internationally…Recent years have seen the emergence of an activist museum practice,

one that seeks to use the resources of the museum to contribute purposefully and actively towards a more fair and just society." [39]

I was convinced that the Museum should stake out a role in the broader social context—the Black Lives Matter movement's response to the rising punitive relationship between Black children, the police and education system. I felt the Museum had a greater calling, even an obligation, to use its voice to stand up to injustices against Black people, particularly youth, and to allow this struggle and consciousness to permeate its mission.

I quickly discovered, however, that my fellow board members did not share my conviction that the Museum could, and should, illuminate a path for society, and cultivate a mission that superseded capital assets. The path I was advocating required a departure from our historic role as a traditional Museum, and this triggered fear in many of my colleagues.

I believe board members must be socially and politically conscious, and must use their knowledge to develop creative and modern strategies to fulfill the organization's mission. This of course is not a question unique to museums: many nonprofit organizations are challenged by the growing volume of demands to scrutinize their relevance. Sadly, however, they often allow fear of change and possible failure to paralyze them, in the process, truly risking irrelevancy.

Sisters and Brothers, I recognize that despite the courage we demonstrate in our daily lives, fear remains a reality for Black people. And this is justified. After all, in

Canada we live, work and play in mainly white spaces. White people do not know Black people, our culture, our language, our value. It is white people who control the majority of what governs our lives, including our charitable endeavours, through government funding and private philanthropy.

"May your choices reflect your hopes, not your fears."

—Nelson Mandela, anti-apartheid revolutionary and president of South Africa

We must be vigilant, because this fear can impede progress, transformation and ultimately freedom. What is the essence of freedom? At its heart, freedom is love. Not the kind of love that is warm and fuzzy and gives you goosebumps and makes you feel good, although it can be that. What I'm talking about is love that intrinsically informs your self-worth, that reminds you of your purpose and tells you the truth of whom you are. Love reminds us of our strength as a people because of what we have survived. A love that proclaims that we are talented and that we harbour many solutions.

∞

"There is no fear in love, but perfect love casts out fear."

—1 John 4:18

At the Museum, I learned that despite the many attempts to kill and erase us, many Black people have survived to give testimony to their lives. My ancestors didn't just survive to hide. They were brilliantly bold. Throughout North America, they built sophisticated organizations and networks like the UGRR and the AME Church with little more than love itself. Twenty years ago, reading Nazrey's meeting minutes and governing documents I learned something that was rarely reflected to me about me. That we as Black people are excellent and continue to demonstrate an infinite love for one another. This I believe empowers us to overcome great obstacles. Make no mistake, it is love that propels me (us) forward, sustains me (us) and gives me (us) hope. Truly knowing this love has no doubt changed me forever. I just couldn't understand why my Brothers and Sisters weren't taking hold of this love.

> *"You've got to learn to leave the table when love's no longer being served."*

> —*Nina Simone, activist, jazz and blues singer*

It was disappointing to realize that my fellow board members did not recognize that to achieve our mission over time required agility and an unwavering commitment to challenge the environment in which we existed and operated.

Nonprofits and charities exist to solve problems. In the case of the Museum, its founder, Melvin "Mac" Simpson, wanted Black Canadian youth to know their worth through history. He wanted them to know where they came from and who they were in a country and world that has largely erased their presence and the contributions of their ancestors. I believe that to maintain and develop Mac's mission over decades requires an adaptation and responsiveness to current realities.

The North American Black Historical Museum was founded in 1975. While we share issues of inequity from the past, we must acknowledge that over the last 45 years inevitably the social and political landscape has evolved. Issues of race and injustice take on a different complexion today. There has been an eroding of civil rights since the '70s, and nonprofits like the Museum need to respond and evolve with the changing times. They should be about more than the bricks and mortar, artifacts and exhibits. In a new role, the Museum should be a beacon of hope and light for Black youth and their co-conspirators who want to learn and assume responsibility for achieving justice and equity.

This cautionary tale is not *just* about the Museum, which is merely one example among many. Issues of modernity and relevance plague many organizations, boards and executive teams in the broader philanthropic sector. In *Decolonizing Wealth*, Edgar Villanueva, argues that,

> *"The field of philanthropy is a living anachronism. It is (we are) like a stodgy relative wearing clothes that will never come back in fashion. It is adamant that it knows best, holding tight the purse strings. It is stubborn. It fails to get with the times, frustrating the younger folks. It does not care."* [40]

When you genuinely care for someone, it is never about you. It is always about the subject of your love. In my household, love was full and plentiful, but it wasn't always easy, and it didn't always feel good. Love is caring and expressions of affection. But it is also about hard truths, accountability, boundaries, challenges, stretching and growing.

Martin Luther King Jr. said,

"Power without love is reckless and abusive, and love without power is sentimental and anemic. Power at its best is love implementing the demands of justice, and justice at its best is love correcting everything that stands against love."

The invitation to join the Museum board in 2010 was a moment of reciprocity. My work began quickly, and I was given responsibility for fundraising planning and strategy. Like any serious fundraiser, I focused on rebuilding relationships in the community and ultimately reintroducing people to the Museum. I began creating plans to re-attract old supporters and new donors to our energetic educational programming and events. And naturally, I began working on a case for support.

After a solid year of renewal and focus, I found myself still stuck on the case for support. In considering the broader context in which I saw the Museum's work, I concluded that the Museum had a larger role to play, a role that pointed us all toward freedom. With the support of the community and an external consultant, we landed on a bold vision that intimidated me and surely many others. Our work was cut out for us. The new vision aligned with Mac's original purpose of supporting the education of Black youth, and the mission challenged and addressed the urgency of the current inequities being faced by so many Black girls and boys. It was a big vision and it was right.

Sisters and Brothers, I believe that courage is just on the other side of fear. If you just wait in the angst a few more moments, courage will emerge. I wish that had been the reality of my experience on the Museum board, because what ensued after the vision was cast was a panic-filled unravelling. Collectively we could not focus on the problem the Museum was created to solve, because the problem had grown, and had become massive and intimidating. I wonder what would have happened if we could have remained in the unease a little longer to allow our courage to rise. What if we could have loved ourselves, our history, our voice more than the fear of failing? What if we had trusted in the collective power of our people?

This experience taught me to commit to the kind of tough love that stands in the face of fear, brutality and strife. I reach for this love to honour the legacy of my ancestors, who cultivated a devotion that refused to surrender in the face of torture, violation, trauma and separation. Descendants of North American slavery were steeped in conflict and catastrophe for generations, yet they managed to emerge with beauty, grace and an abundance of love. Our ancestors knew great fear, yet still they fought for love and dared to taste freedom. I am sustained in my quest for justice and freedom in the nonprofit sector by understanding the history of the love of our ancestors.

Black love should be writ large. Its power transcends oppression and abuse, and is boundless. There were 14

generations of slavery in the United States and 8 generations of slavery in Canada. Black people were in bondage
for nearly half a millennium and still, we emerge with
empathy and love for ourselves and others. Slave families
were mercilessly dispersed by the system, but our love
drove mothers to never stop searching for their children,
brothers to never stop seeking their sisters and husbands,
their wives.

The influential AME Church newspaper, *The Christian
Recorder*, was one newspaper that published "Information
Wanted" advertisements from Black people desperately
looking for family members sold away during slavery,
even 50 years after slavery ended.

∞

*"INFORMATION WANTED By a mother
concerning her children. Mrs. Elizabeth Williams,
who now resides in Marysville, California was
formerly owned together with her children, vis:
Lydia, William, Allen, and Parker, by one John Petty,
who lived about six miles from the town of Woodbury,
Franklin County, Tennessee. At that time, she was the
wife of Sandy Rucker, and was familiarly known as
Betsy, sometimes called Betsy Petty.*

*About twenty-five years ago, the mother was sold
to Mr. Marshal Stroud, by whom, some twelve or
fourteen years later, she was, for the second time
since purchased by him, taken to Arkansas. She has
never seen the above-named children since. Any
information given concerning them, however, will be*

gratefully received by one whose love for her children survives the bitterness and hardship of many long years spent in slavery." [41]

∘∘∘

The basic love bond between mother and infant is fundamental to human existence, and there is no stronger human connection. Yet this was the very bond targeted and broken by slave owners through the commodification of Black children, mothers and fathers. I stand in awe of the failure to eradicate the Black family during slavery, and the fact that it could not exhaust the love that remains for lost loved ones. My family and I continue to search for our lost ancestors, even today.

"I looked for the approach of another gang in which my wife was also loaded with chains. My eye soon caught her precious face, but, gracious heavens! that glance of agony may God spare me from ever again enduring!…I seized hold of her hand while my mind felt unutterable things…I went with her for about four miles hand in hand, but both our hearts were so overpowered with feeling that we could say nothing, and when at last we were obliged to part, the look of mutual love which we exchanged was all the token which we could give each other that we should yet meet in heaven."

—*Henry 'Box' Brown* [42]

It is almost supernatural that we as Black people do

not hate white people for the pillaging of our hearts, our children and our lives over centuries. Instead, we refined a unique and expansive capacity for love.

Still, despite the reign of terror that slavery spawned and no matter how much it altered and disfigured black marriages, it did not and could not annihilate them—or the love that sustained them. African Americans proved relentlessly creative and resourceful in building marriages and kinship ties that functioned for their survival. We should never lose sight of the depth of feelings and affection that undergirded these relationships and the sacrifices they were willing to make for the sake of preserving them. [43]

The expressions of love and power in our culture, our music, art and poetry, have permeated and influenced the broader cultural fabric of North America.

∞

"Those embers of Africanness that joy kept alive in subversion and resistance through music, dance and religion birthed what we now recognize as the broader American culture. The first spirituals evolved into gospel and morphed with Anglo- and Irish-American folk songs to produce 19th-century American popular music. The ring shout and buck-and-wing led to America's first dance crazes between 1870 and 1930, including the cakewalk, the foxtrot and tap dancing.

Quite simply, there is no American joy, no American

*culture, without Black joy, and no Black joy without
Black pain from and resistance to American racism
and exploitation."*

—*Donald Earl Collins, American University* [44]

∞

Although in Canada Black people are fewer in number
than African Americans in the United States, we have also
shaped the essence of culture in Canada. And similar to
our American Brothers and Sisters, our cultural contributions have been ignored and erased.

Robin Allot, author and linguistic scholar, says that
"love is a total state of organization," and I agree. With
our immense legacy of love, I think back on my time at
the Museum. I regret that collectively we were unable to
draw from our ancestors the strength to go beyond the
fear of the unknown and reach for our rightful place in
the struggle for freedom. I regret that my fellow Black
Museum colleagues didn't dive into the ocean of love
that is our legacy to be reminded that we have something meaningful and powerful to share, and that our
voice matters and justice and equity can only be achieved
when Black people are centred in the struggle. Indeed,
in the centre of the struggle is our rightful place. Those
regrets, however, will not allow me to forget that I come
from a love that never stops searching for our love. And
I will always allow the richness of empathy to drive my
compassion so love will rise and face fear.

Brothers and Sisters, we must meet the moment; you

have something precious to share, and it is rooted in a rich tradition of love. Our historical context gives us a unique capacity to wade in the deep waters of tragedy, opposition and change. We bring this inherent power into our organizations and the charitable sector. Do not let the fear of continued exclusion and humiliation stop you from stepping out and raising your voice. What we possess is rare, and the charitable sector needs us. Our goal is not simply the success of the individual. The goal is our collective freedom. I want Black people to be free.

Savannah Blue in her poignant poem, *Slave Love*, speaks of the deepest love imaginable,

> I still sees tears
> rolling down his bruised cheeks
> Tragedy flavoured his lips whispering:
> 'Now go pray for our chillin.'
>
> Owz luv is owz only freedom. [45]

Beloved, may the infinite love of our ancestors reign in your hearts and permeate your lives and reach your organizations, so that society can meet freedom. And fear will no longer govern.

Yours until love and freedom reign,

Your Sister, Nneka

►●◄

Nneka Allen is a Black woman, a descendant of the Underground Railroad, an Ojibwa of Anderson Nation, a Momma and a sixth-generation Canadian and the principal and founder of The Empathy Agency.

Expressions of Gratitude

The editors are thankful to each other for the memories made during the creation of *Collecting Courage*. This work brought us together, deepened our bond, our sisterhood and our friendship. We will always remember this narrative journey of affirmation, truth and love. Thank you to Rochelle Sodipo, with Roseredd Etc, for sharing her creative insight and artistic guidance for the book cover design. Thank you to Adrian M. Williams for contributing his artistic talent to this project and for bringing the book cover to life. We admire and celebrate your generosity and your spirit.

Nneka's Gratitude

Blessings come in a myriad of forms. For me, these gifts are delivered through beautiful relationships with my family and friends.

In the front row of my life is the most courageous confidante, defender and truth-teller. To my Aunt, Madame Justice Beth Allen (of the Ontario Superior Court), your example of brave grace is a perpetual teacher. Thank you for patiently walking with me and gently calling me higher. Your devotion to me in this writing project and my life is extraordinary and my gratitude abounds.

***

To my Momma, Karla Taylor, you were the first to show me how to love people. You taught me how to create and invest in the community. Your example is emblazoned in my mind and grafted on my heart.

***

To my Dad, Michael Allen, thank you for always celebrating the fire in my belly. You introduced me to the charitable sector. You showed me I could change the world. You are the reason I am an activist fundraiser.

***

To my brother Din, I celebrate your philanthropy. You have always cared deeply about your community.

***

To my daughter Destiny, you are my greatest inspiration. Your light always illuminates my path. I write for you. I fight for you. I stand for you. I cherish you. To Skylar, my son-in-law, thank you for your dedication to me and my work, it is a beautiful outpouring of your love for Destiny. When the pages of my life end, I know that you two will be one of the most brilliant chapters.

***

To my life-long friends Jackie, Jodi and Andrew, and to the newest addition Nicole, the reciprocity in our relationships is spirit-lifting, soul-satisfying and joy-inducing. You are family to me and your presence in my life is a gift.

***

And to my Uncle Dwight (aka Dog Bone- Smack Head,

as my young daughter called him), thank you for ensuring I always reach my destination, for the early morning laughs, the dance-offs, the play fights and for always standing-in. You lighten the load.

My joy overflows because of what each of you deposit in my life. With fierce love and gratitude, I recognize you. Thank you!

Camila's Gratitude

I am so fortunate to have amazing supportive family and friends.

***

Dad — Jose Luiz Nunes Pereira, J.D. you are such an inspiration! Your eagerness for knowledge is my drive to always keep learning. Thank you for the countless conversations we had throughout this process; for sharing with me your brilliant insights and priceless words of wisdom.

***

Mom - Zulma Vital Nunes Pereira, your courage to always speak up and challenge the status quo is my true motivation to speak and share my truth. With you I learned the power of community and community transformation. You dared to dream to give black children better education and opportunities. Your dream is still alive after over 30 years (Monte Carmelo Community Association, Sao Paulo-Brazil) and changing communities and children's lives. Being part of and living your dream fuels my commitment to the non-profit sector.

***

My siblings and best friends—Munirih Pereira Giuzio and Luis Felipe Vital Nunes Pereira, PhD, CFA. Even from a far we are always together and connected more than ever. Thank you for always challenging me and being there to brainstorm with me; your voice is unique! Our countless conversations always filled with jokes and laughs have helped me to cope with many stressful moments; you are my confident!

***

To the one that keeps me going, my husband—Adrian Williams; thank you for the many conversations we have had, many times about the same things over and over again…thank you for the many edits, all your input and invaluable advice as I navigated through this process. There is no one better than you who knows my stories; you have been there with me when I cried, when I celebrated, and when I was uncertain of many things. You are always here with me and often reminds me of why I do what I do. Thank you so much for everything; I couldn't have done this without you.

***

To my friends, who have been there for me through ups and downs, who inspire me to keep working in what I believe in, who I have shared many stories with and have encouraged me along the way—thank you!

***

To my sister-friends and editors—Nicole and Nneka; what an adventure! Thank you for the several hours we spent together; for the fun and songs (so many lol) that resulted from our many meetings and conversations. And this is just the beginning...I am thrilled for what is yet to come.

***

I love you all!

Nicole's Gratitude

I couldn't ask for more than what my late parents, Wesley & Jessie Salmon, poured into me my entire life—nurtured love, fed curiosity, a cradle of safety and security and a cocoon for me to just be me without prevailing dictates of whom a little girl should be or should like to do. I live each day to honour you the way you honoured and blessed me—with confidence, caring, kindness and respect for others—always. And Mom, I am finally doing what you have always told me—"Nicky, you have so many things to offer, you need to write." Better late than never and Mommy, I know you are laughing because you have the last word.

***

To my six siblings whose lives have taught me both good and painful life lessons and specifically to my sisters Bonita and Marjorie, my brothers Bosville and Mark, you have all been that constant in my life and I can't imagine a me without you—your baby sister loves you and still looks up to you. To my sisters-in-law Dona (my legal eagle guide throughout this process) and Marcia (a.k.a Molly), you know you are really my sisters; end of.

***

To my nieces and nephews (and their families) who have been a constant in my life — Shana, Uhuru, Amanda, Sarah, Bosville II, Charles, Shivonne, Jason and Jonathan — thank you for the privilege of being your Momti (somewhere between an Auntie and Mommy), a role I treasure beyond description or measure. To my niece and nephew-in-laws Andrea, Brent, Shauna and Yohannes and my honourary nieces and nephews (you all know who you are so don't have to ASK), you are family and so appreciate being part of your lives — I love you. And for my four great nieces and four great nephews (and others left to come), I hope you will be inspired to walk good in this life and to always do so with courage.

***

To my friends, many from my childhood and many who I met as work colleagues, I treasure our friendship, through the good, the fun, the painful and challenging moments we have shared. Thank you Bonita, Marjorie and my friend Beverley Knott for reviewing and giving me feedback on my poem *Come, Take a Walk with Me*. Finally, to my two co-editors Nneka and Camila, what a wonderful adventure it has been working on this book together. You are both 'beyond excellent' and you are forever my BBBS (Beautiful, Brilliant, Black Sistas).

Nuff love!

To the Contributors

Simple gratitude is not enough for the emotions that have washed over us, swept us up and sat us down when reading your testimonies. The vulnerability exposed in your voices is buoyant at times, graphic and complicated in others but, in the end, intimate. The sacrifice each author made to realize this work is truly philanthropic. In fact, at this moment, we know it is sacred. Each story breaks open truth, lays bare the pain and pulls back the veil so we can see our healing, our tenacity, our excellence.

We must acknowledge the current social and political racial injustices that we are surviving, with the persistent killings of Black bodies in Canada and the United States at the hands of police. As Black people, many of us have suffered illness and loss due to the COVID-19 virus. Some of us are struggling with the loss of jobs, going through a process of taking care of family members or recovering from physical injuries.

And still with courage we write.
And we dared to share our hearts.
And we give you our mastery.
This is a precious gift.
And a serious warning.

With great respect, devotion and love,
Camila, Nicole & Nneka.

BIOGRAPHIES

Olumide (Mide) Akerewusi, CSR-P, CDEP
Ontario, Canada

Mide is a proud husband and father to two young adults. He is passionate about equity and social justice, and possesses an avid interest in current affairs and global politics. Mide is a British-born African living in Canada. He obtained a B.Sc. (Hons) degree in Business Studies and Sociology from the University of Surrey, and an M.Sc. (Econ) in the Political Economy of Asia and Africa from SOAS, University of London.

Mide is Founder and CEO of AgentsC Inc., a Canadian-based international company delivering equity philanthropy and social research services to the nonprofit and private sectors. He has worked in senior relationship fundraising roles and consulted for a number of the world's leading nonprofit organizations.

With more than 25 years' experience as a philanthropy expert, Mide currently serves on the Board of 100 Strong, a charity helping young Black boys achieve excellence and academic attainment through mentorship by Black male leaders.

Nneka Allen, CFRE
Ontario, Canada

Nneka is a Black woman, a descendant of the Underground Railroad, an Ojibwa of Anderson Nation, a Momma and a sixth generation Canadian. Born in the '70s, Nneka was raised during a time of Black power and acute political awareness in North America. As a lover of justice, Nneka has inspired philanthropy as a Fundraising Executive in the charitable sector for the last 20 years. She is the principal and founder of The Empathy Agency, where she helps organizations deliver more fairly on their mission and vision by coaching leaders and their teams to explore the impact identity has on organizational culture and equity outcomes. Nneka is also a founding member of the Black Canadian Fundraisers Collective.

Nneka's ultimate joy is her daughter Destiny, an Environmental Scientist working with Indigenous communities in British Columbia. Together Destiny and Nneka continue their family legacy of philanthropic activism in Canada.

Naimah Bilal, CFRE
Ohio, USA

Naimah is a Washington DC native, nonprofit leader, and fundraising executive. Drawing inspiration from her prior career as an orchestral musician and symphony programming executive, Naimah has spearheaded wide-ranging efforts for the Cincinnati Symphony Orchestra, the Cincinnati Waldorf School, and the University of Cincinnati where she serves as Director of Foundation Board Relations. In this hybrid role she manages a spectrum of enterprise governance efforts and manages a major gift portfolio. Naimah launched *Bawse With A Cause*, the first podcast devoted to profiling the stories, perspectives, and insights of black and brown executives in the nonprofit sector. She is a co-host of Urban Consulate Cincinnati, a national platform for exchange on topics of equity and racial healing. She received her BA and MA at Indiana University Bloomington and Case Western Reserve University. She is now pursuing her mba with a concentration in Economics at the University of Cincinnati.

Christal M. Cherry, MA
Georgia, USA

Christal is a nationally recognized nonprofit executive and professionally trained fundraiser. With over 20 years in the nonprofit sector, she has supported higher education institutions, human services organizations, and faith-based missions. Now as CEO of The Board Pro, a consulting firm designed to transform leaders through board service, she customizes training and support for the unique needs of each client. She earned an MA in Counseling from Hampton University, a BA in Liberal Arts from Hofstra University, and multiple professional development certifications. She currently serves on the board of the Greater Atlanta chapter of the Association of Fundraising Professionals and the Villages of Carver YMCA. She is on faculty at candid where she teaches courses in fundraising and board development. She also is a member of the African American Development Officers Network, Toastmasters, and F3, Fabulous Female Fundraisers, which she founded.

Nicole E. Cozier

Virginia, USA

As a queer, Black woman and an immigrant, Nicole's career path has often been a reflection of her own quest for liberation. Nicole has more than 25 years of experience as an advocate, trainer/facilitator, and social justice leader and champion in the direct service, advocacy and philanthropic  sectors. Whether the focus of her work was reproductive health and rights, women's economic empowerment, or LGBTQ+ equality, intersectionality, equity, inclusion, and justice has always been central to her work. Because, in the words of Audre Lorde: "There is no such thing as a single-issue struggle, because we do not live single-issue lives." Nicole is currently leading the equity and inclusion work at a US-based national LGBTQ civil rights organization. Nicole was born in Barbados, grew up in Toronto, and now lives in Northern Virginia with her wife and daughter. She is undergraduate alum of the University of Toronto and graduate alum of Temple University.

Sherrie James, CFRE
Ontario, Canada

Sherrie James is a fundraising executive with more than 18 years' proven success in development, marketing, project management and event management. She has worked within various sectors including health and social services. She is currently the Director, Philanthropy at Luminato Festival Toronto. She serves on the board of Generation Chosen, an organization committed to helping the youth of our communities who are being denied equitable opportunities to succeed in life.

Sherrie is a proud mother of two amazing and beautiful kids. Her daughter and son are her teachers and her inspiration. When not fundraising or learning from her kids, Sherrie can be found listening to the sweet sounds of soca and reggae, reading, or bingeing k-dramas on Netflix.

Fatou Jammeh
Ontario, Canada

Fatou is a passionate human rights advocate and fund development professional. She has worked in various fundraising capacities for several organizations including Doctors Without Borders (MSF), UNICEF Canada, The Match Fund, and the Women's Legal Aid Centre. She is personally committed to promoting diversity and inclusion in all spaces and is on a trek to change the face of philanthropy. Actively engaged in community initiatives, she leads the Bridge Gambia Platform, Afropolitan Canada and is the Community Lead for Manyatta Network. Fatou holds a Bilingual Degree in International Studies from York University and a Certificate in Inclusion and Philanthropy from AFP Canada. She is enrolled in the Nonprofit Management Certificate at George Brown College. Fatou has lived and worked in Canada, Tanzania, France and Gambia and speaks English, French, and Mandinka.

Muthoni Kariuki, MNPL, CFRE
Ontario, Canada

From childhood, Muthoni fell in love with nonprofits working alongside her parents, who valued the power of giving back to the communities they lived in. Her parents instilled in her that our lives become meaningful through the impact we make on others, more so than living and working just for ourselves. Muthoni's lived experience as an African Canadian Professional Fundraiser, mother, and community advocate informs her desire for equity, inclusion, and social justice, and for the last decade, she has been advocating for a more just and equitable Canadian fundraising sector. She is a Certified Fund Raising Executive, holds an Honours Bachelor of Science B.Sc. (Hons.) degree from the University of Toronto and a Master's degree in Philanthropy and Nonprofit Leadership (MPNL) from Carleton University. When Muthoni isn't fundraising, she spends her most important, valued time with her family.

Heba Mahmoud, MBA
Virginia, USA

Heba is a mission-driven professional committed to creating an inclusive, diverse, and equitable professional sector that welcomes and engages underrepresented communities. She has spent the last fourteen years working with membership associations. Heba serves as the senior manager of diversity initiatives at the Consumer Technology Association, where she is responsible for building and implementing initiatives to advance inclusion in the tech ecosystem. Previously, she worked at the Association of Fundraising Professionals, where she took the lead in launching the *Women's Impact Initiative*, a program committed to creating an impact by breaking down workplace barriers. Heba holds a Bachelor of International Business and Marketing from Howard University and an mba from Strayer University. Heba is also a scholar in the 2018-2020 class of the American Society of Association Executives' Diversity Executive Leadership Program. She is passionate about youth engagement and actively volunteers with several DC area groups.

Niambi Martin-John
Ontario, Canada

Niambi is a social change champion, community developer, advocate and empowering partner who has dedicated her career to increasing capacity for marginalized, racialized and at-risk communities. With a career spanning over 20 years, Niambi has committed her talents in fund development, strategic planning, grant writing, executive training and teaching to grow revenue and mentor emerging leaders in the arts, social service and health charity sectors.

She currently teaches in the nonprofit Leadership Management Post Graduate Diploma Program at Seneca College and provides mentorship and coaching services to nonprofit boards, volunteers, and staff.

Kishshana Palmer, CFRE
New York, USA

Kishshana is a uni-mom, trainer, educator, author and professional speaker. She is the founder of Kishshana & Co., a global management and leadership learning company. Kishshana is the author of *Hey, I'm New Here* and founder of The Rooted Collaborative, a global learning community for Black, Indigenous and women of color leaders in the social sector. When she is not starring in the *Life of My Queenager* (okay it's not a real show, but it could be), she is dropping knowledge about leadership and life. Kishshana is the epitome of your classic '90s Queens homegirl and quintessential corner office executive. She is your daily dose of Claire Huxtable with a side of Blanche Devereaux.

Camila Vital Nunes Pereira, PhD
Ontario, Canada

Born and raised in Brazil, Camila comes from a very mixed family including Black, Spanish, Italian, Portuguese and Native Indian. She understood from a very young age that race relations, identity and gender roles were central not only to her family but to herself, and that skin color in Brazil dictates your role, future and existence within society. Since childhood Camila has been involved in philanthropy through her family's community initiatives. Her career in the nonprofit sector is a means to contribute towards the eradication of all forms of prejudice preventing the advancement and betterment of humankind, and she is a fundraising professional in Toronto and a coach to Brazilians involved in philanthropy and fundraising in Brazil and Canada. Camila holds a PhD in Public Policy/ Public Administration & International Relations from Howard University. Alongside her career, Camila keeps a strong connection with her family in Brazil and loves spending time with her husband Adrian and cat Lila and travelling.

Nicole Salmon
Ontario, Canada

Shaped by her Jamaican identity and deeply influenced by spending two-thirds of her life in Canada, Nicole is a skilled communicator who embraces her natural curiosity and thirst for variety and new challenges. An avid reader, gardener, sports enthusiast and mentor, Nicole is anchored by family, committed to service, building connections and deepening personal relationships.

Spending over twenty-five years working in the non-profit sector managing a variety of fundraising portfolios, in 2014 Nicole founded Boundless Philanthropy, a fundraising consultancy providing a range of services, including interim leadership, board and leadership development. She is a former Director of Fund Development at Oxfam Canada.

She serves on the Boards of Realize, an organization working to improve the lives of people living with hiv and other episodic conditions, and WellFort Community Health Services. A Book Review Panelist with The Charity Report Literary Hub and an inspired member of a Black Canadian Fundraisers Collective.

Birgit Smith Burton
Georgia, USA

Birgit Smith Burton is the executive director for Foundation Relations at Georgia Tech. She is a respected leader in the fundraising profession and a well-regarded speaker on the topics of fundraising and diversity. She has authored articles and co-authored books including *The Philanthropic Covenant* with Black America, and recently, received the Council for Advancement and Support of Education's 2020 Opportunity and Inclusion Award. As the current chair-elect for the Association of Fundraising Professionals' global board, she will serve in 2023 as the first African American woman chair in the organization's 60-year history. She serves as board chair for the A.E. Lowe Grice Scholarship Fund and Hosea Helps. Birgit founded the African American Development Officers Network, which provides professional development and networking opportunities for fundraisers of color. A member of Alpha Kappa Alpha Sorority, Birgit earned her BA in media communications from Medaille College in Buffalo, New York.

Marva Wisdom, MA
Ontario, Canada

Marva is a leading voice in Canada on empowering social change and is a committed social justice advocate. She is a respected and popular facilitator, moderator and speaker on equity, and inclusivity. Marva's skills, talent and experience have contributed to significant projects, including  as outreach director for the Black Experience (Research) Project (Environics Institute), as Lead Advisor for the City of Guelph's award-winning Community Plan, and Director of Musagetes Foundation's ArtsEverywhere Festival.

Her volunteer leadership spans three decades including the YM-YWCA, United Way, Guelph Black Heritage Society, Canadian Centre for Diversity, Operation Black Vote Canada, and Rotary. Marva's recognitions include the Queen's Diamond Jubilee Medal, the YWCA's Woman of Distinction Award and the University of Guelph's Lang School of Business, Alumni Award. Marva holds a Master of Arts in Leadership and is a Senior Fellow at the Munk School of Global Affairs and Public Policy (University of Toronto).

Endnotes

1 https://www.huckmag.com/perspectives/opinion-perspectives/n-i-g-g-e-r/

2 Dimel, B. R. (2016). *Engaging the Line: How the Great War Shaped the Canada-US Border*. Vancouver: UBC Press.

3 Marsh, J. (2009). Updated 2020. Railway History in Canada. The Canadian Encyclopedia.

4 Farrow, A. et al (2006). *Complicity: How the North Promoted, Prolonged, and Profited from Slavery*. Ballantine Books.

5 Trudel, M. (2013). *Canada's Forgotten Slaves: Two Hundred Years of Bondage*. Vehicule Press.

6 Skolnik, M. (1990). Continental Divide and the Ideological Basis for Differences in Higher Education between Canada and United States. *Canadian Journal of Higher Education.* 20(2): 81-93).

7 The Charity Report (June 17, 2020) Charity, Philanthropy and the Structures of Racism. (https://www.thecharityreport.com/features/charity-philanthropy-and-the-structures-of-racism/).

8 Akinsete, K. K. (July 6, 2020) The Importance of Journaling Black Life During Extraordinary Times. (https://blavity.com/the-importance-of-journaling-black-life-during-extraordinary-times?category1=opinion).

9 George William Cooke, composer (1925). I've Got the Joy, Joy, Joy, Joy, Down in my Heart.

10 Alex Comfort (1972) *The Joy of Sex*

11 Du Bois, W. E. B. (William Edward Burghardt), 1868-1963. (1968). *The Souls of Black Folk*; essays and sketches, p. 52. Chicago, A. G. McClurg, 1903. New York :Johnson Reprint Corp.

12 Villanueva, E. (2018). *Decolonizing Wealth: Indigenous Wisdom to Heal Divides and Restore Balance*. Oakland: Berrett-Koehler.

13 Assimilation is *"the process by which a minority individual or group gives*

up their own identity by taking on the characteristics of the dominant culture." William Little, Introduction to Sociology: 2nd Canadian Edition. Retrieved from https://opentextbc.ca/introductiontosociology2ndedition/chapter/chapter-11-race-and-ethnicity/#section11.3.

[14] Ibid.

[15] *Covering, Assimilation, and Code-Switching: A Quick Guide.* (2019). Eskalera. (https://eskalera.com/2019/03/04/covering-assimilation-and-code-switching-a-quick-guide)

[16] Hewlin, P. (2020). How to Be More Authentic at Work. *Greater Good Magazine*, August 3, 2020.

[17] Microaggression can be a statement, action, or incident regarded as an instance of indirect, subtle, or unintentional discrimination against members of a marginalized group such as a racial or ethnic minority. (https://www.dictionary.com/browse/microaggression?s=t)

[18] Stevenson, B. (2014). *Just Mercy: A Story of Justice and Redemption*, 1st ed. New York: Spiegel & Grau.

[19] No Name in the Street

[20] Koyenikan, I. (2014). *Wealth for all Africans: How Every African Can Live the Life of Their Dreams.* Grandeur Touch.

[21] Wolfenstein, E. V. (1993). *The victims of democracy: Malcolm X and the Black revolution.* London: Free Association Books.

[22] Alberta Civil Liberties Research Centre: Understanding Whiteness. (http://www.aclrc.com/whiteness)

[23] Kivel, P. (1996). *Uprooting Racism: How White People Can Work for Racial Justice.* p. 19. New Society Publishers.

[24] Henry, F. and Tator, C., 2006. *The Colour Of Democracy: Racism In Canadian Society.* pp. 46-47. 3rd ed. Toronto: Nelson.

[25] Estable, A., Meyer, M., & Pon, G. (1997). *Teach me to thunder.* p.21. Margin: Ottawa.

[26] While recognizing the numerous definitions available, for the purpose of context and clarity in this narrative, I have created a definition of "equity" that is more applicable to the subject matter of my narrative.

[27] Generosity in Canada and the United States: The 2017 Generosity Index, Fraser Institute; (www.fraserinstitute.org)

[28] Fundraising Around the World: NFP Synergy, More Strategic, 2019. (https://nfpsynergy.net/free-report/charity-fundraising-around-the-world

#downloads)

[29] Taylor, S. L. *(1998). Lessons in living. Anchor.*

[30] The Invisible Man, movie

[31] Ibid.

[32] The best universities in Brazil are public (besides very few) and free of charge; private universities are expensive and usually with inferior level of education

[33] Brazil was the last country in the world to abolish slavery in 1889. No public policies were created at that time.

[34] Private education in Brazil is much better quality than public education

[35] Rhimes, S. (2015). *Year of yes: How to dance it out, stand in the sun and be your own person.* Simon and Schuster.

[36] Freire, Paulo. *Pedagogy of the Oppressed. Penguin Education, 1972.*

[37] Villanueva, E (2018). *Decolonizing Wealth: Indigenous Wisdom to Heal Divides and Restore Balance.* p. 163. Oakland: Berrett-Koehler.

[38] Brown, Adrienne M. *Emergent Strategy: Shaping Change, Changing Worlds.* AK Press, 2017.

[39] https://museumsandmigration.wordpress.com/2016/07/21/social-role-of-museums-new-migrations-new-challenges/

[40] Villanueva, E (2018). *Decolonizing Wealth: Indigenous Wisdom to Heal Divides and Restore Balance.* Oakland: Berrett-Koehler.

[41] http://informationwanted.org/items/show/1

[42] The story of Henry Brown, popularly known as Henry "Box" Brown, who escaped slavery by having himself shipped in dry goods crate from Richmond to Philadelphia.

[43] https://www.history.com/news/african-american-slavery-marriage-family-separation

[45] https://apple.news/AitVkj7RfRS-RfE62tGPhyQ

[45] https://www.houstonpublicmedia.org/articles/arts-culture/2017/04/28/198143/video-national-poetry-month-a-slaves-love-by-savannah-blue/

Book Group Discussion Questions

1) What did you know about the experiences of Black people working in the charitable sector before you read *Collecting Courage*?

2) These authors have provided a perspective on charities that you don't usually hear about. How has it affected your view of charitable work?

3) What were your initial emotional responses as you read about the experiences shared in the book?

4) Upon completing the book, did you experience a shift in your emotions? If yes, can you describe the shift?

5) Do the experiences described resonate with you in any way, either as someone who has had similar experiences, someone who has observed incidents as described in the book, or someone whose conscious or unconscious behaviors may have caused harm to a Black colleague or employee?

6) Now that you have read the book, what and how do you plan to use the information? What will change for you?

7) The book features contributions from fundraisers in Canada and the US. In the introduction, co-editor Nneka Allen shares the context and history of both countries. Were you surprised by the information shared in the introduction? What surprised you most?

8) The essays are divided into four themes – Joy, Pain, Freedom, Love. What do you believe are the significance of the themes and why do you think the editors structured the book in this way?

9) If you had to write under one of these themes to describe your work, school, or volunteer experiences, which theme would you choose, and why?

10) What central message(s) do you take away from the contributions under each of the themes?

Also Available from Rootstock Publishing: